AIM FOR THE MOON

Moon phases

Photo shapes

By Mary Kei

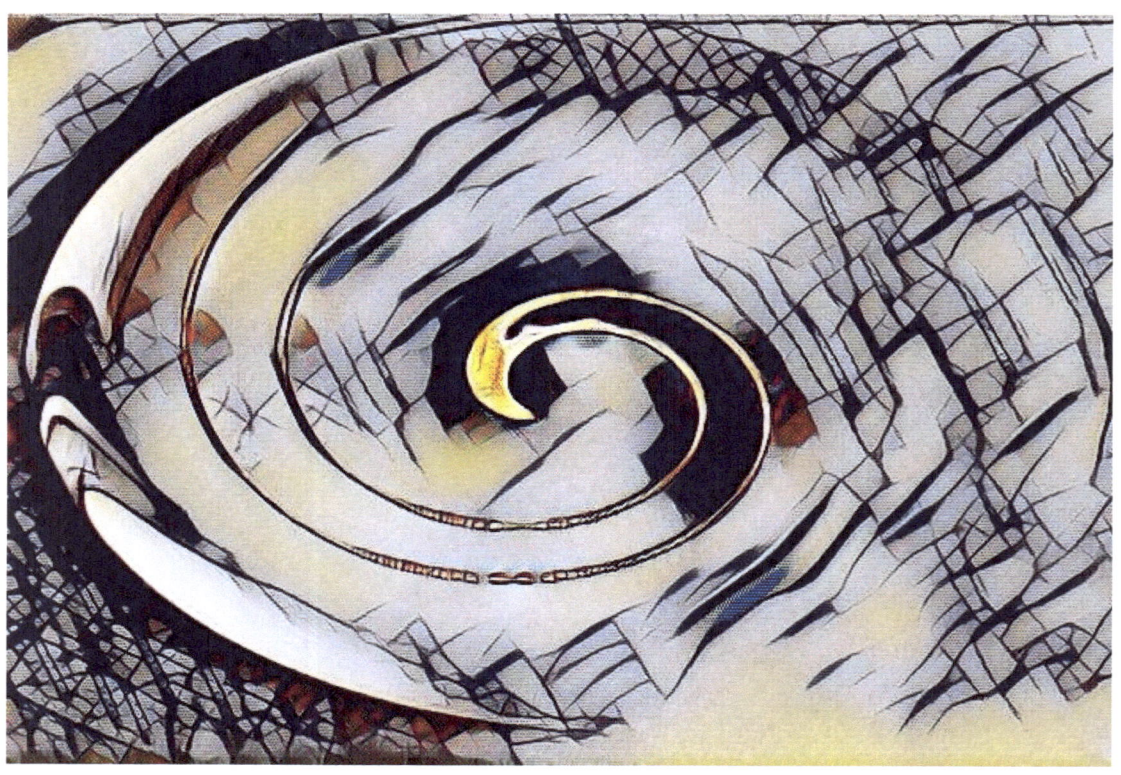

Saturn and crescent moon

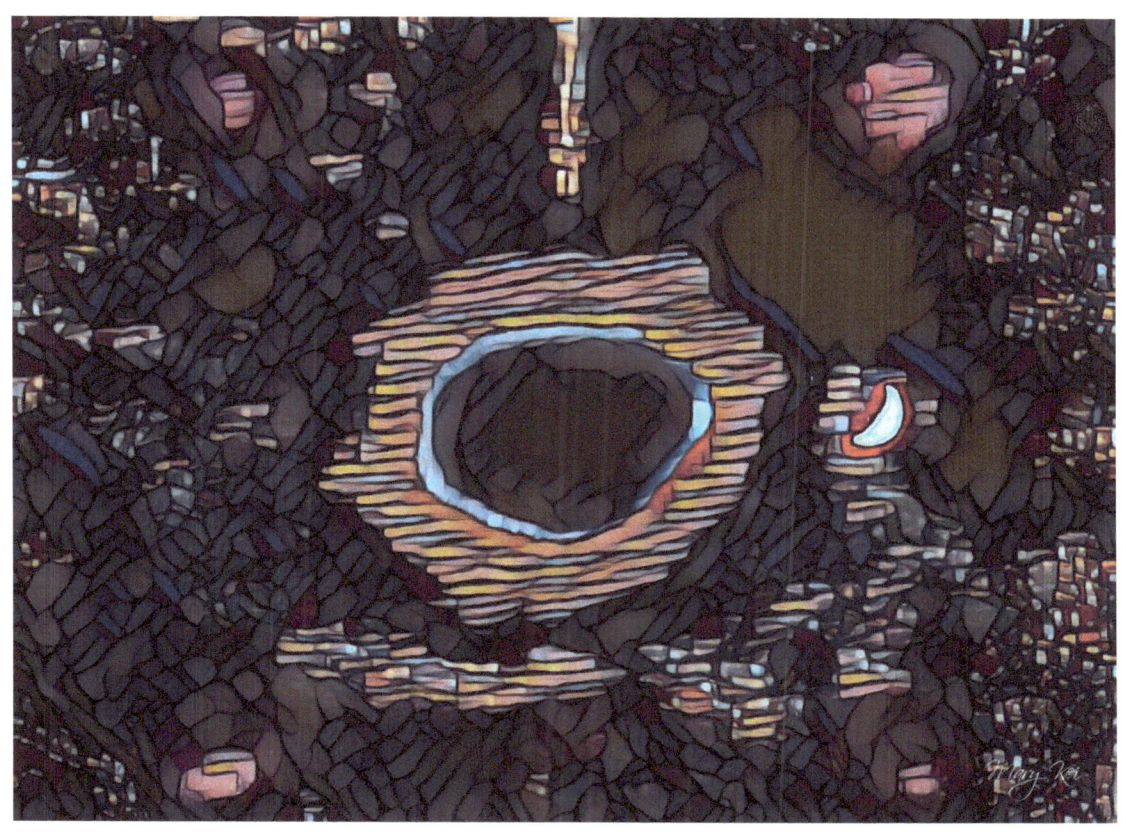

Moon and city lights

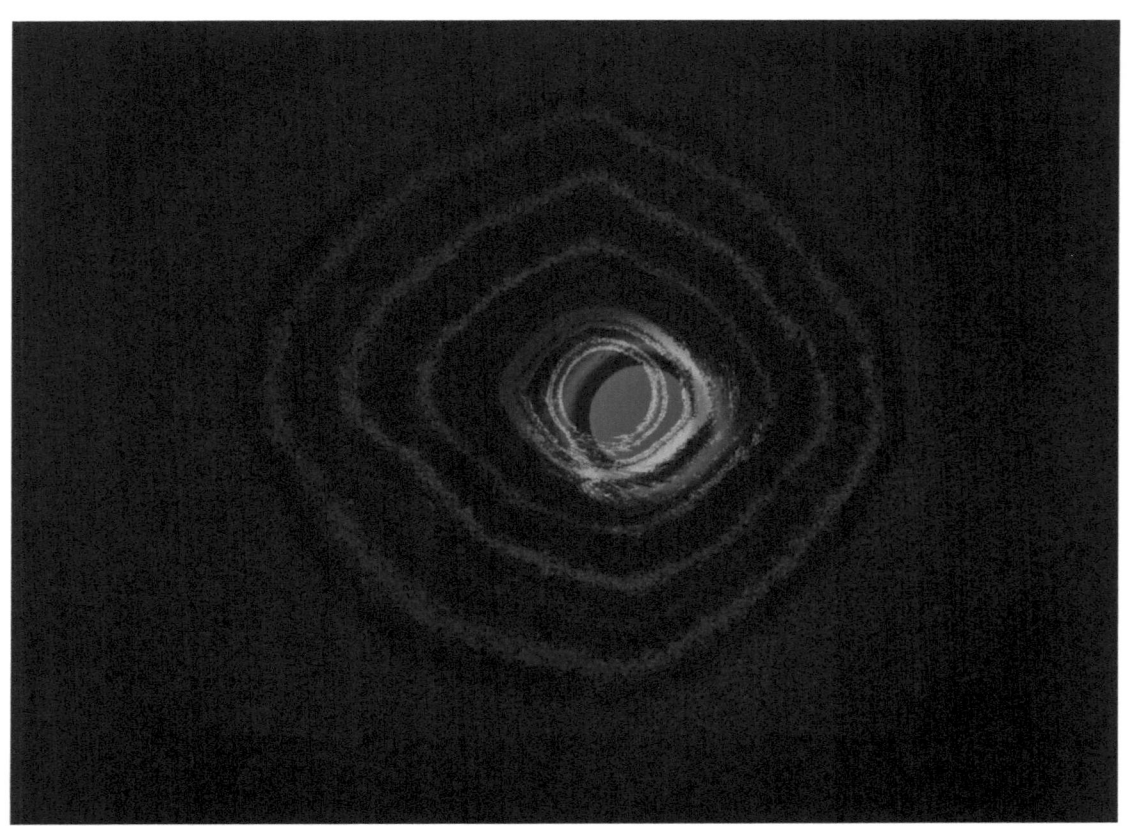

Moon' s eye

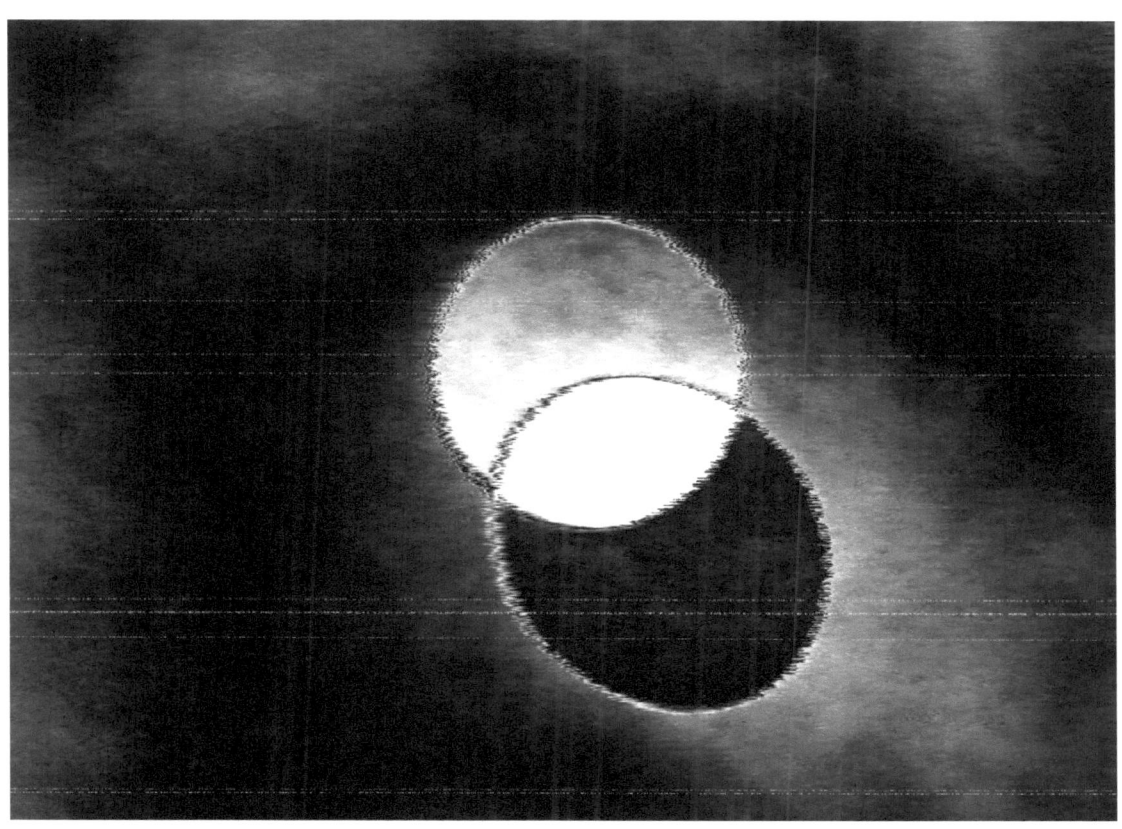

Lilith – The dark side of the moon

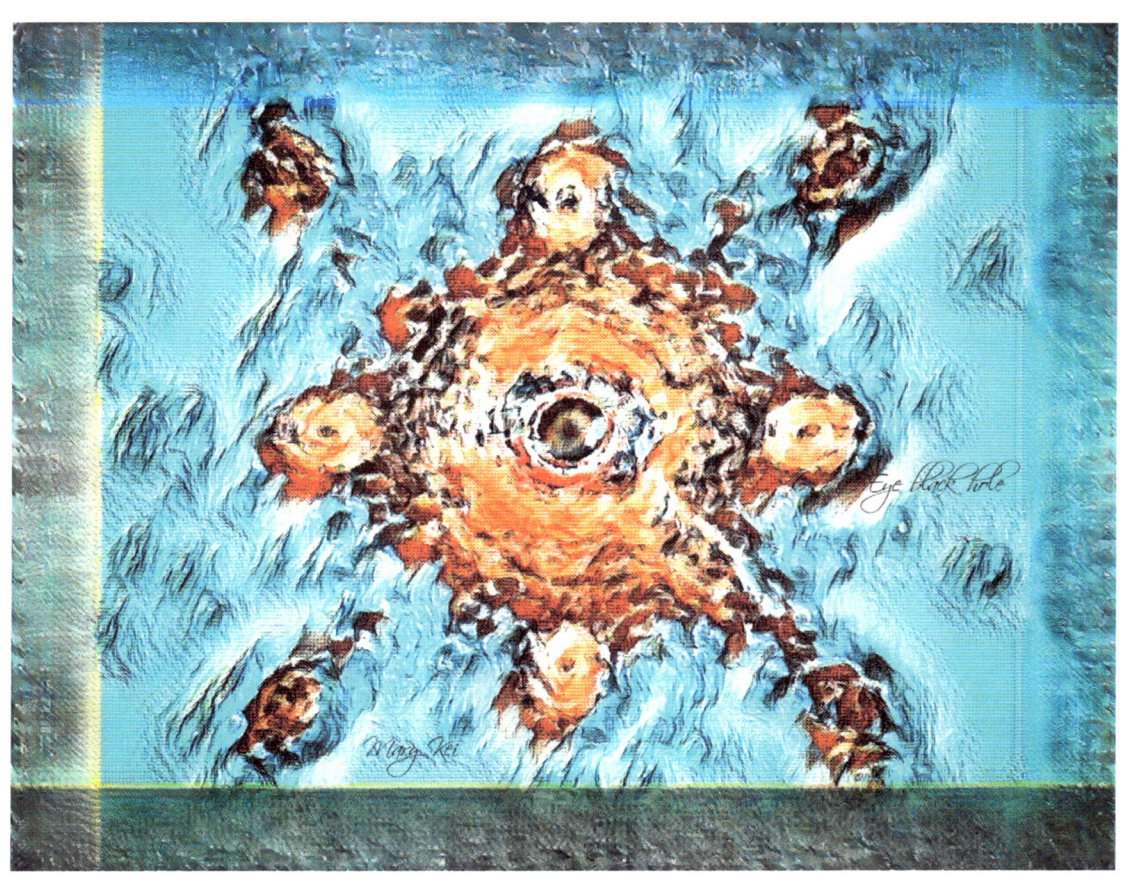

Moon' s eye black hole

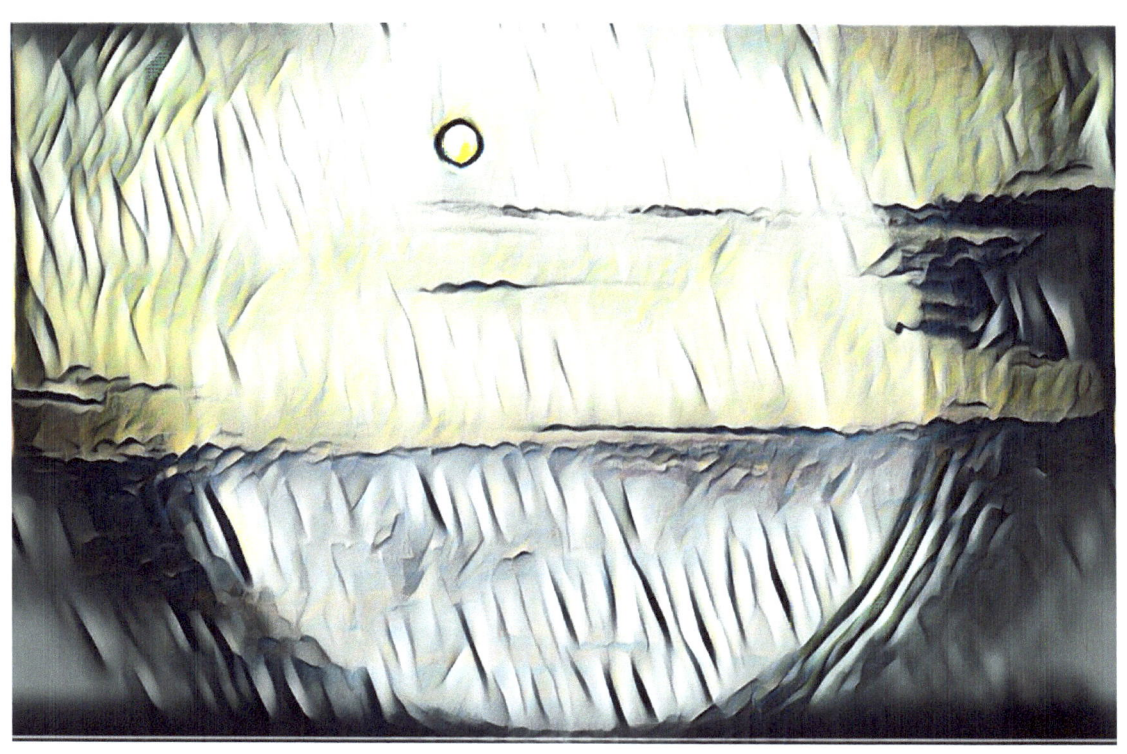

Moon' s aurora

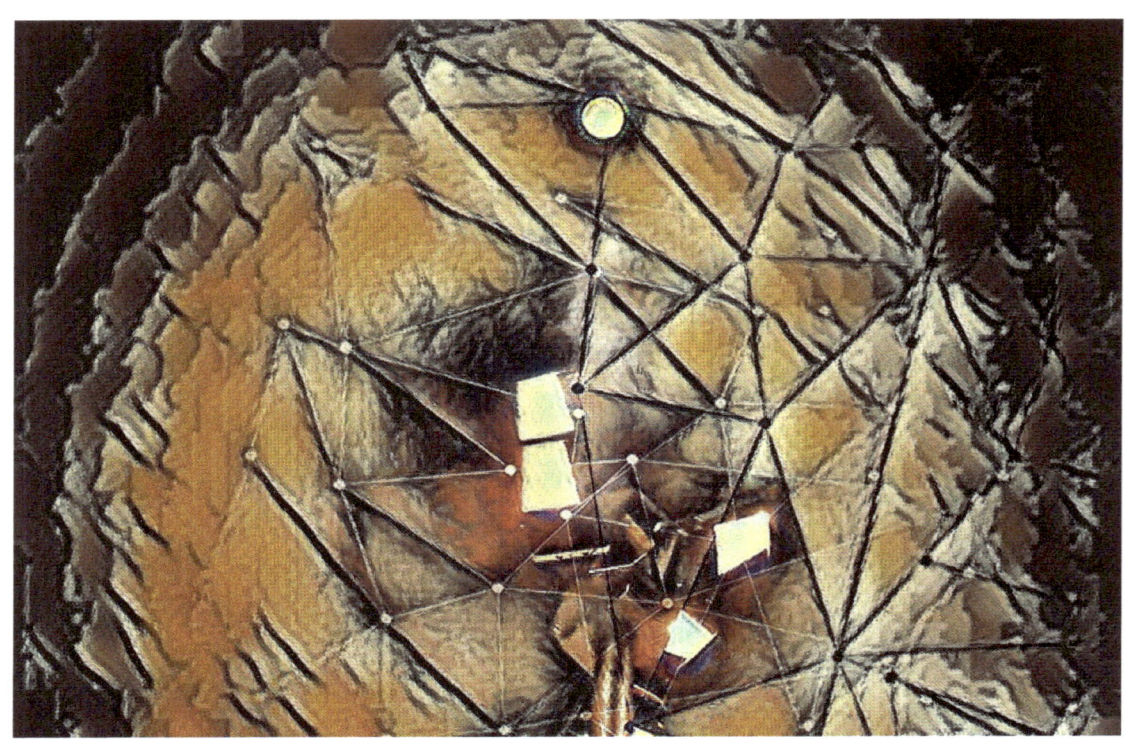

Wolf city moon

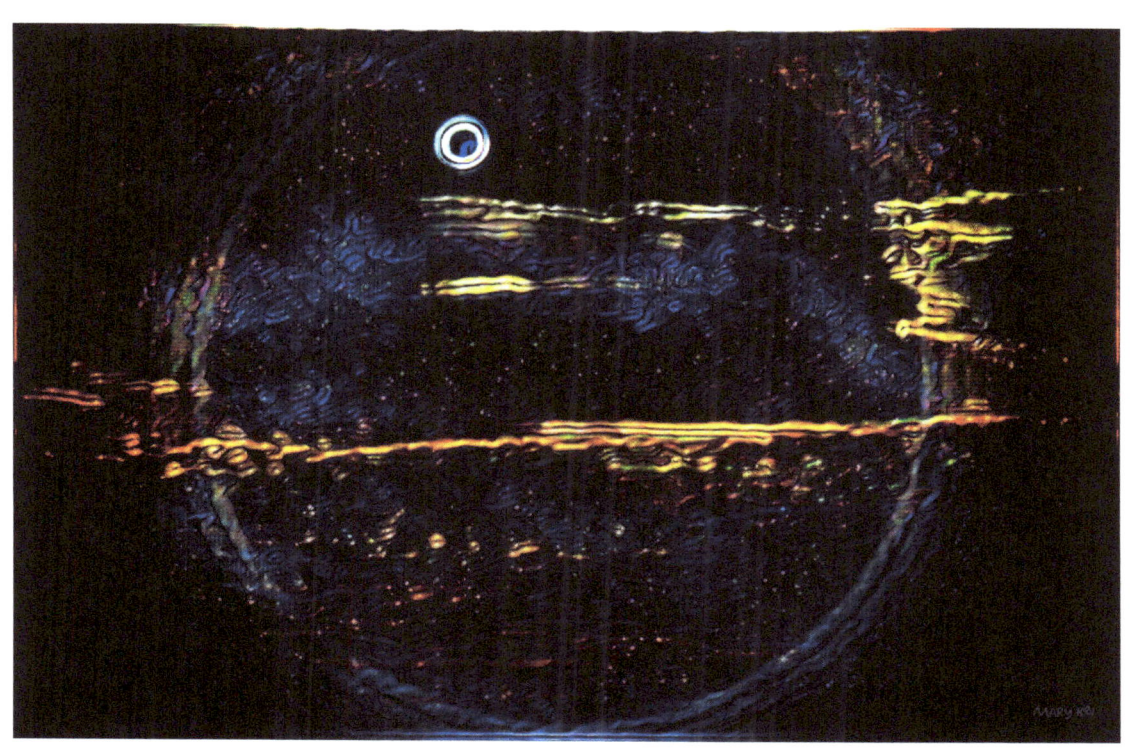

August fool Moonset

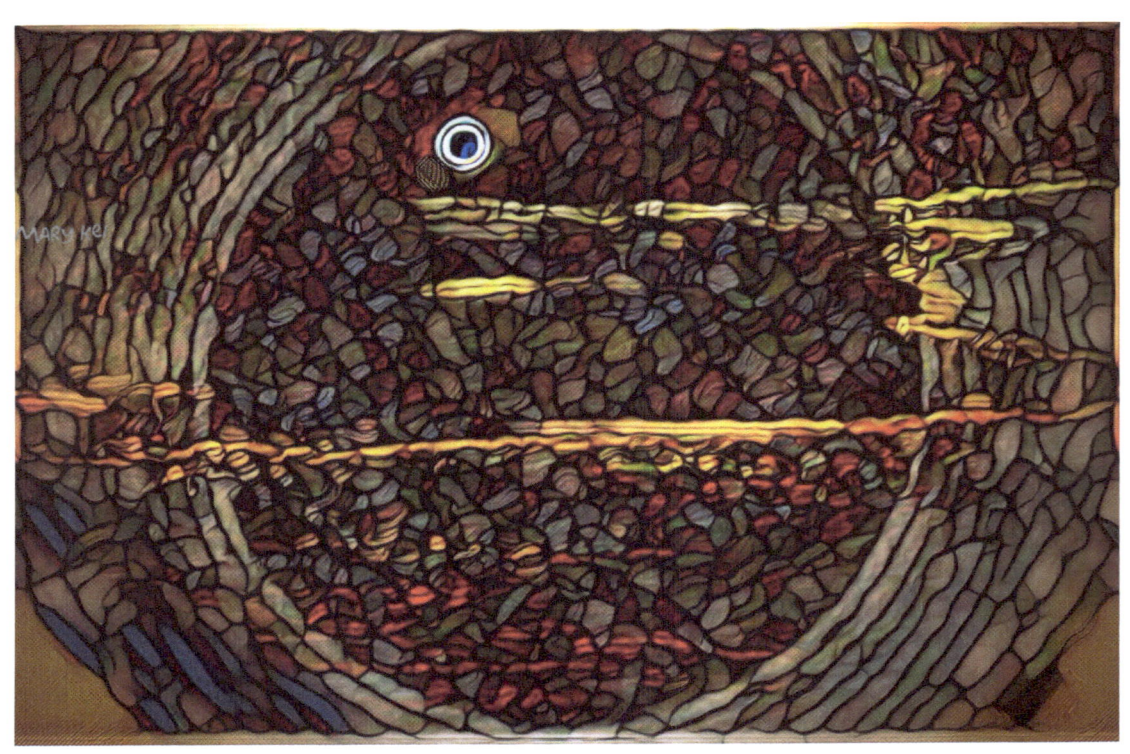

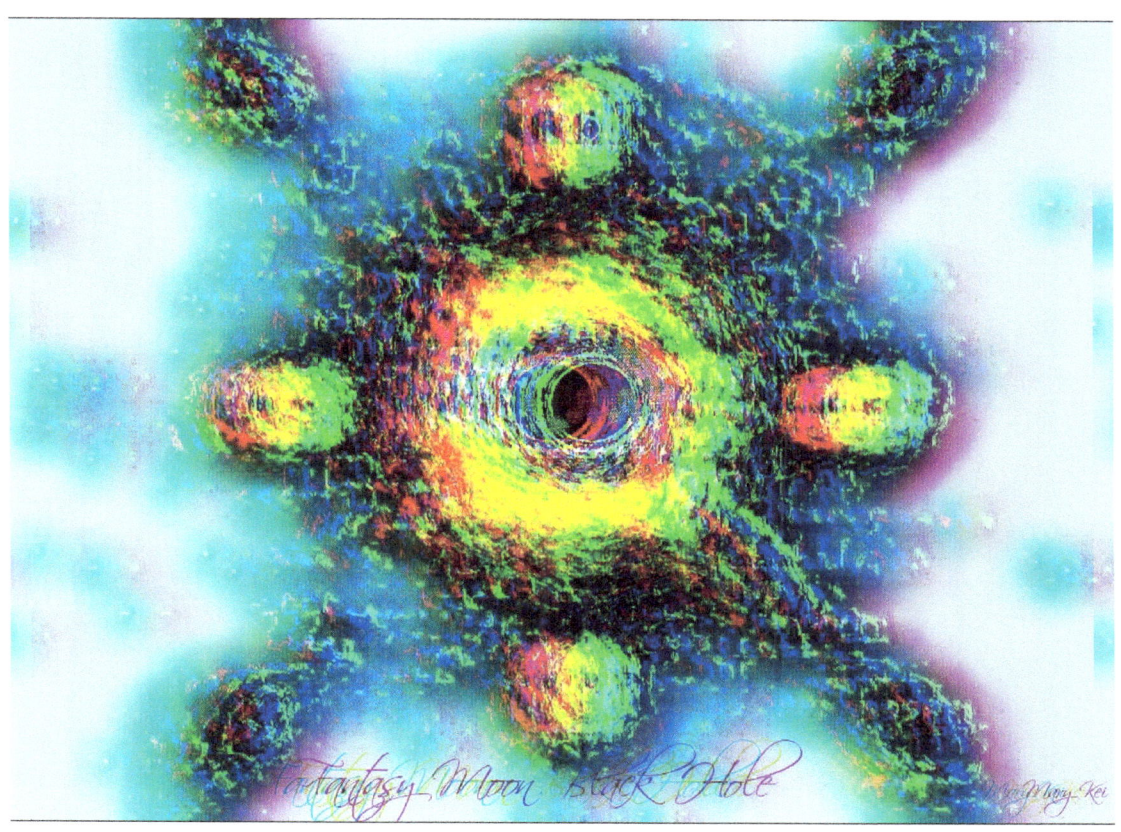

Fantasy moon black hole

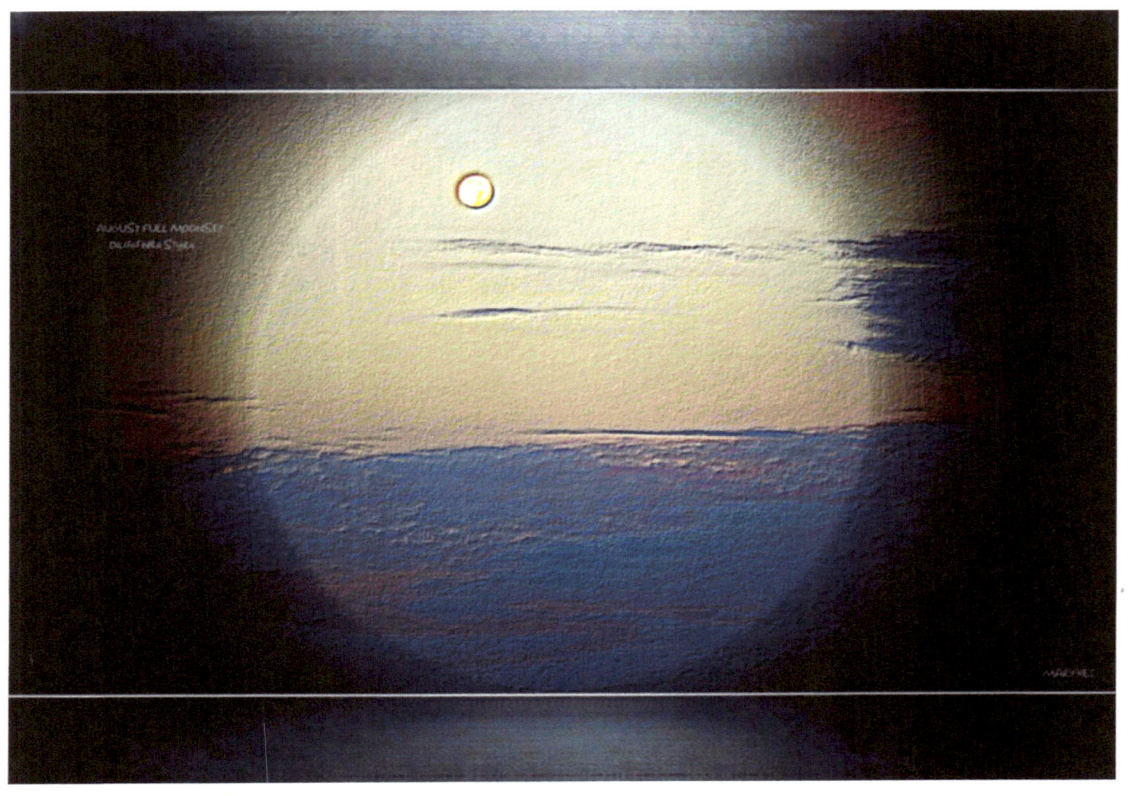

August fool moonset

Dilisos Nea Styra

Greece

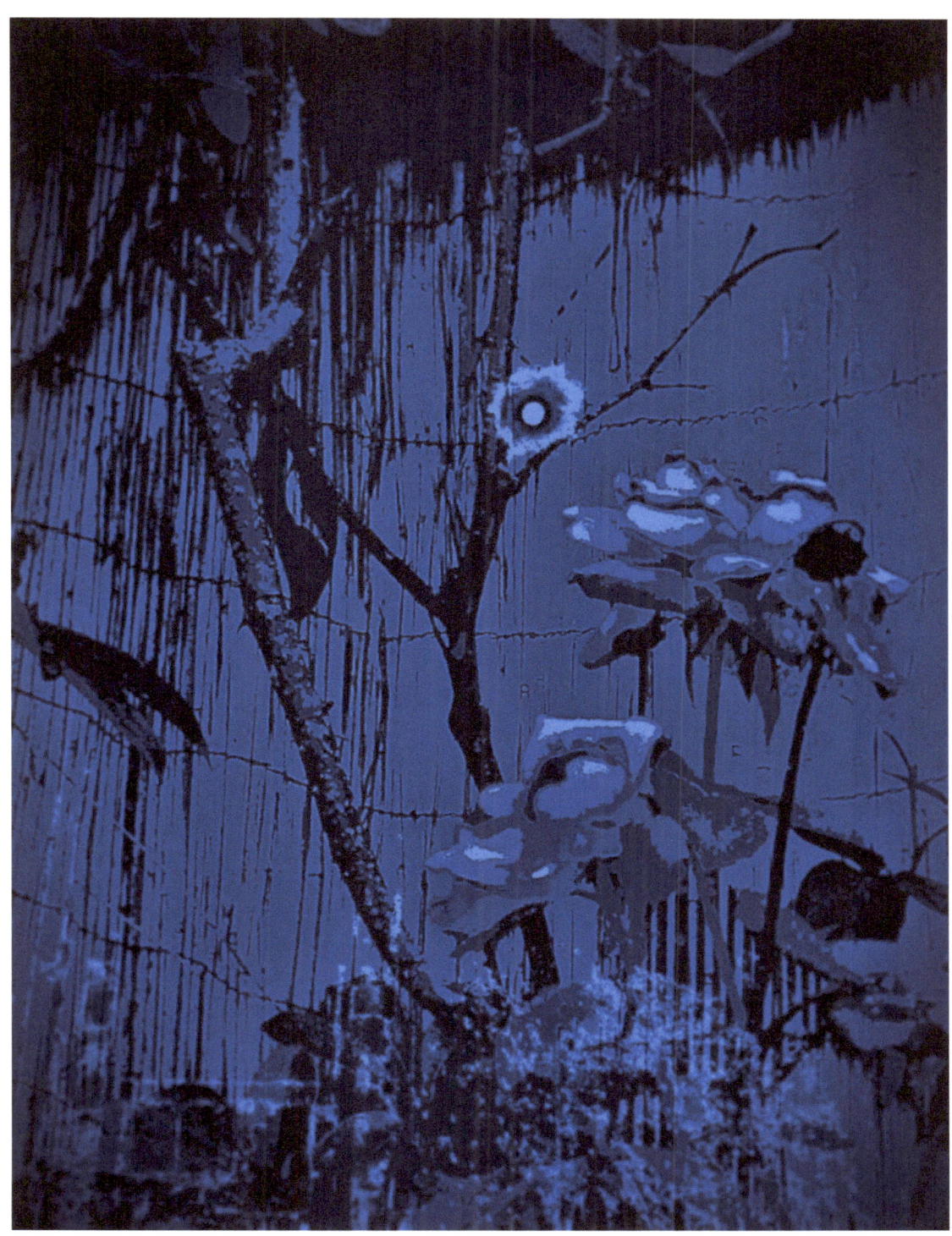

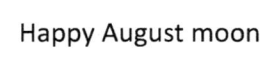

Happy August moon

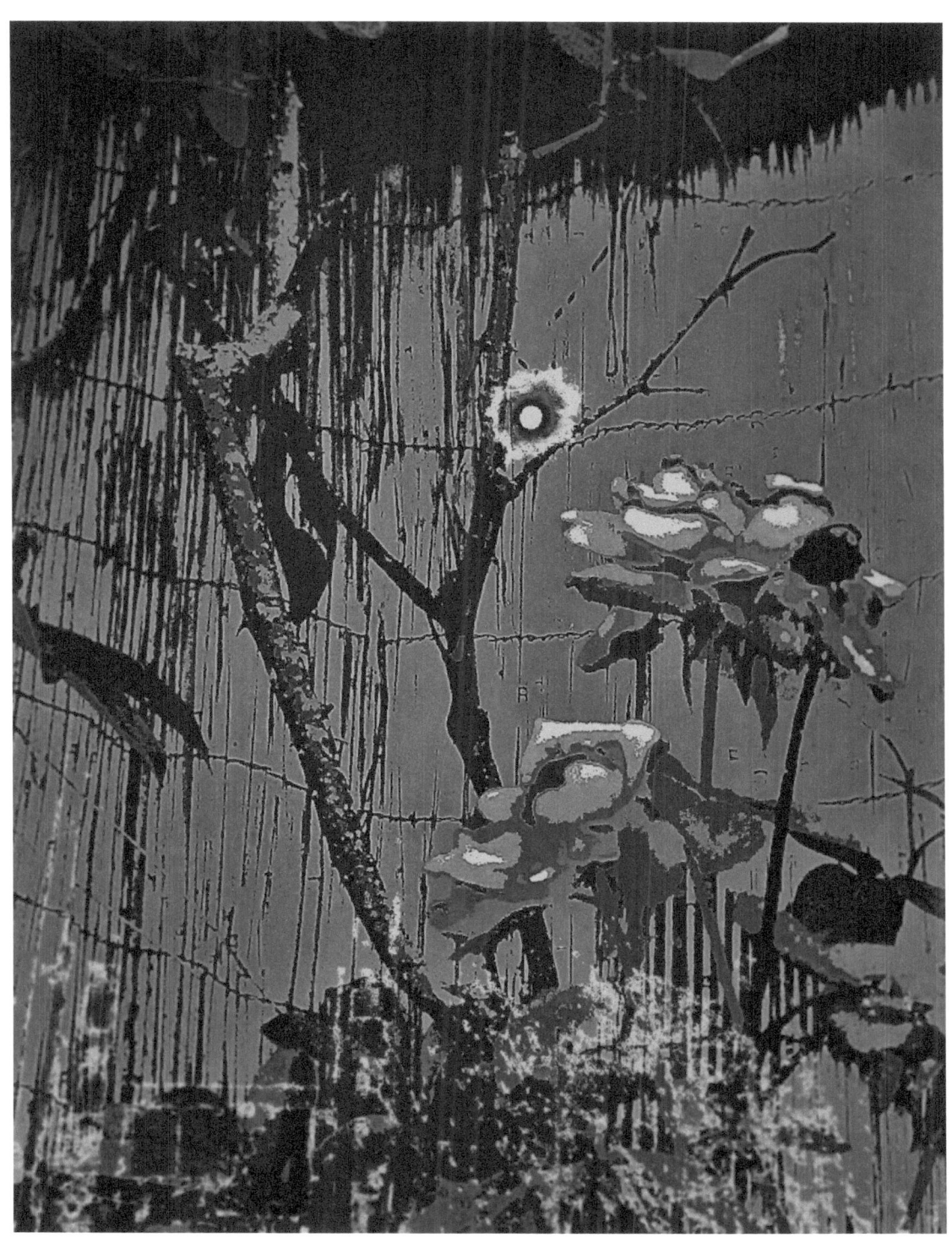

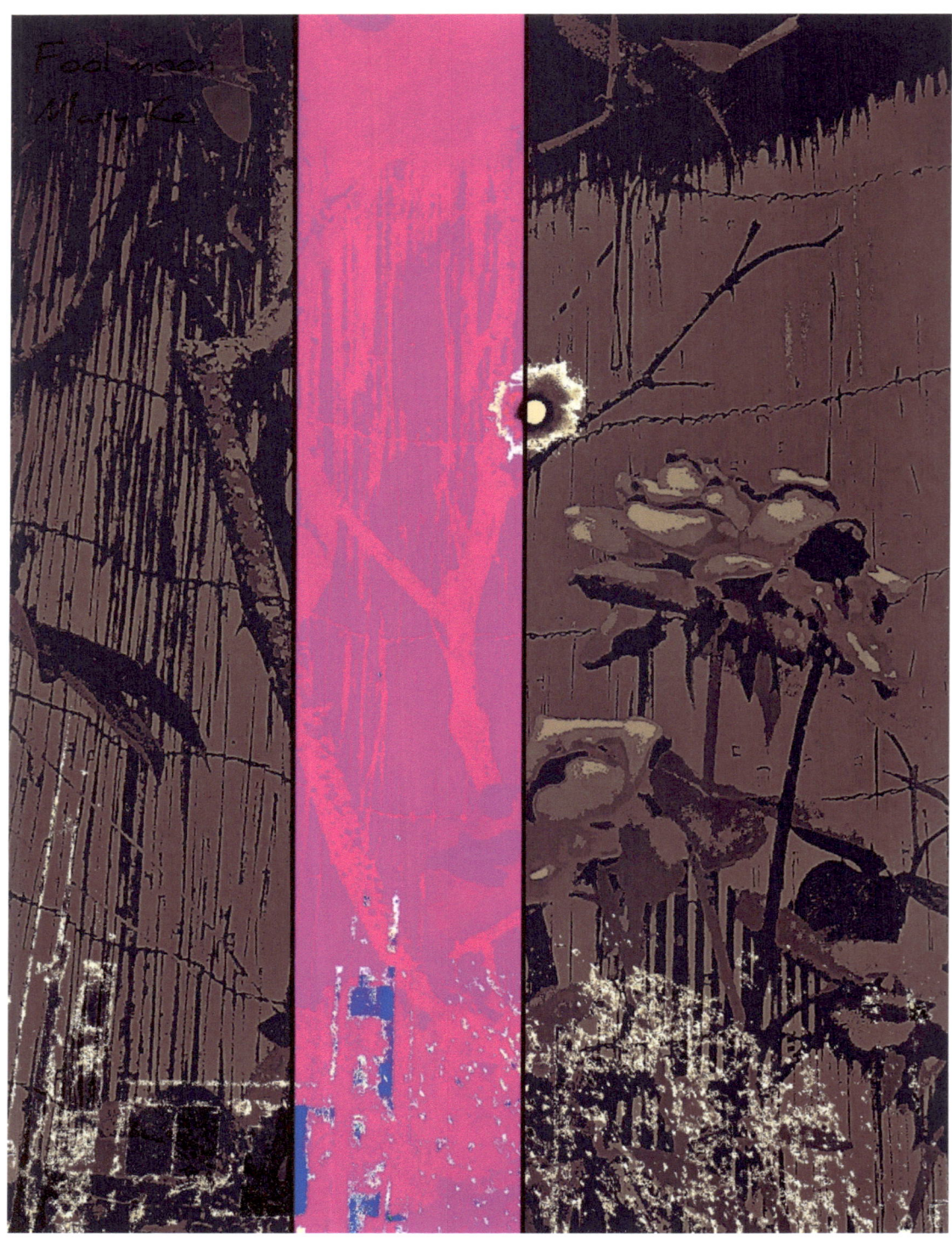

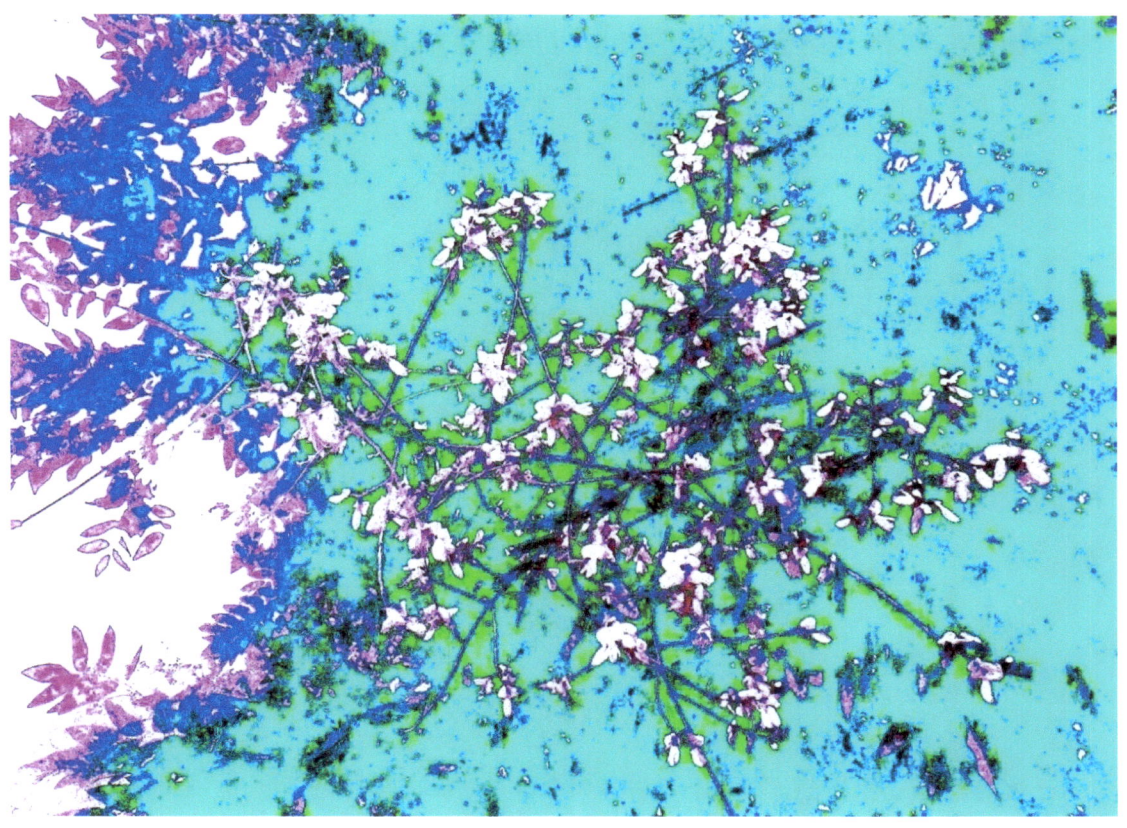

Moon lost in dreams

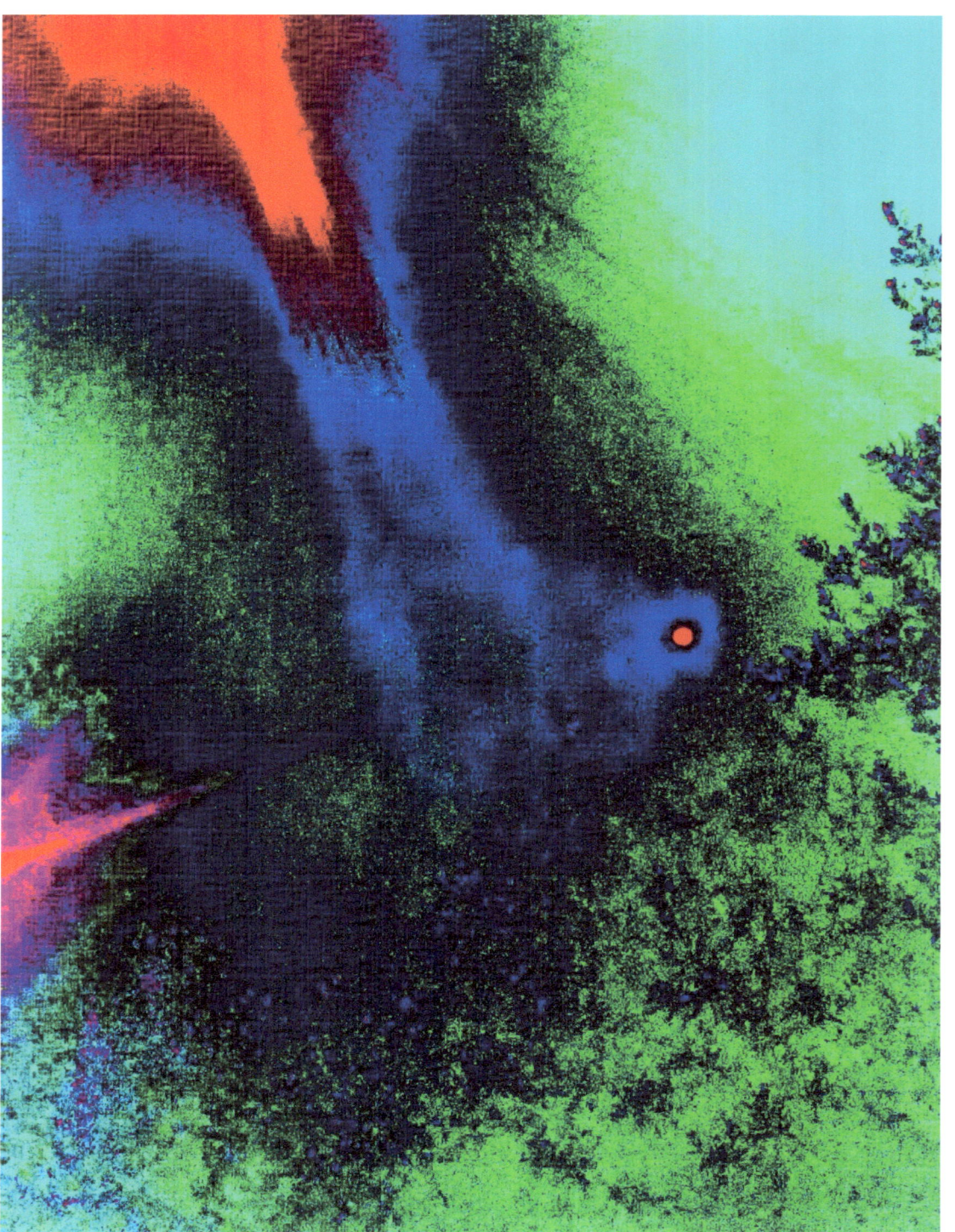

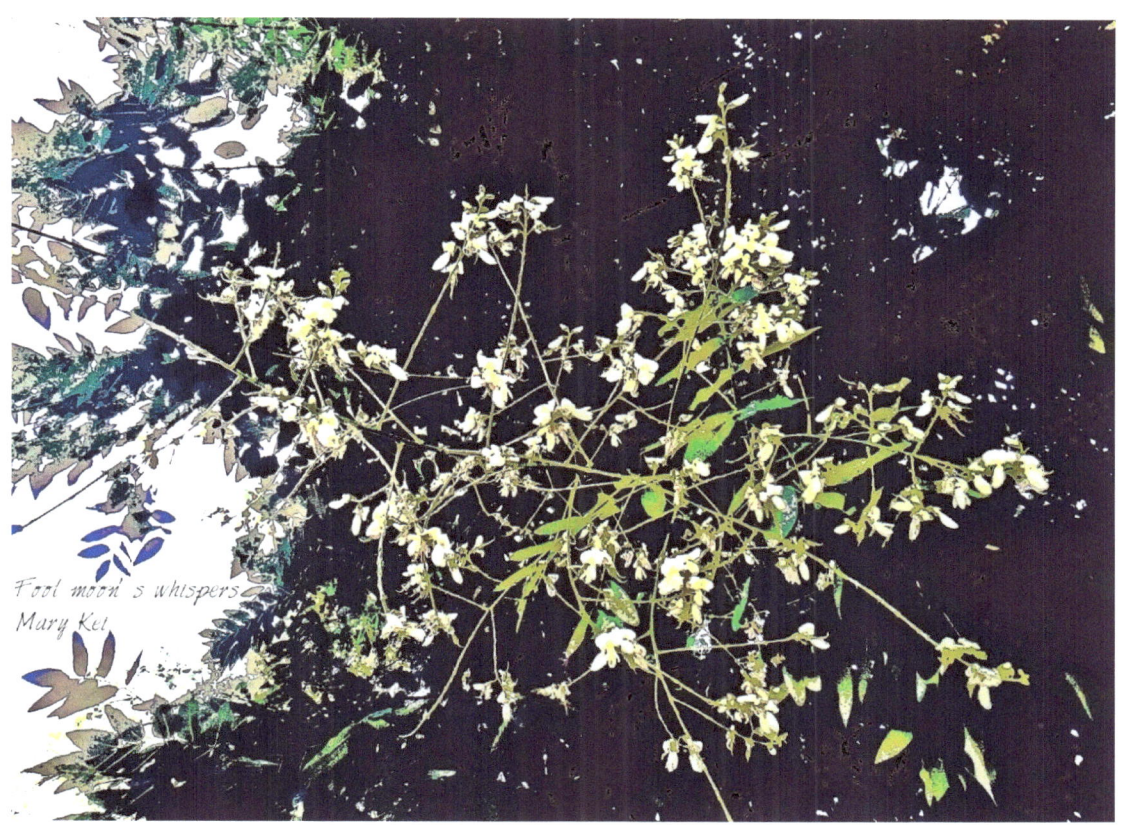

Fool moon's whispers

Mary Kel

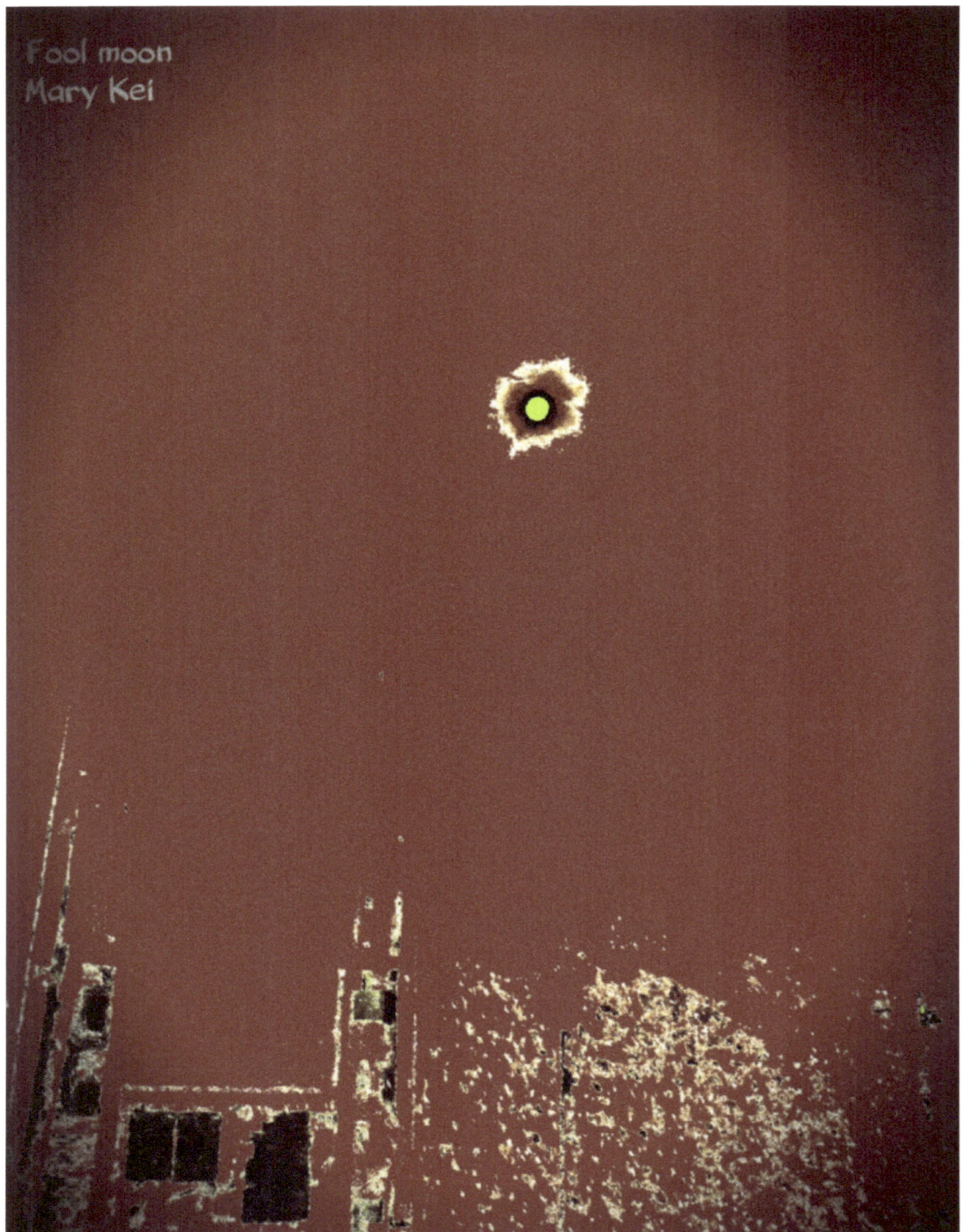

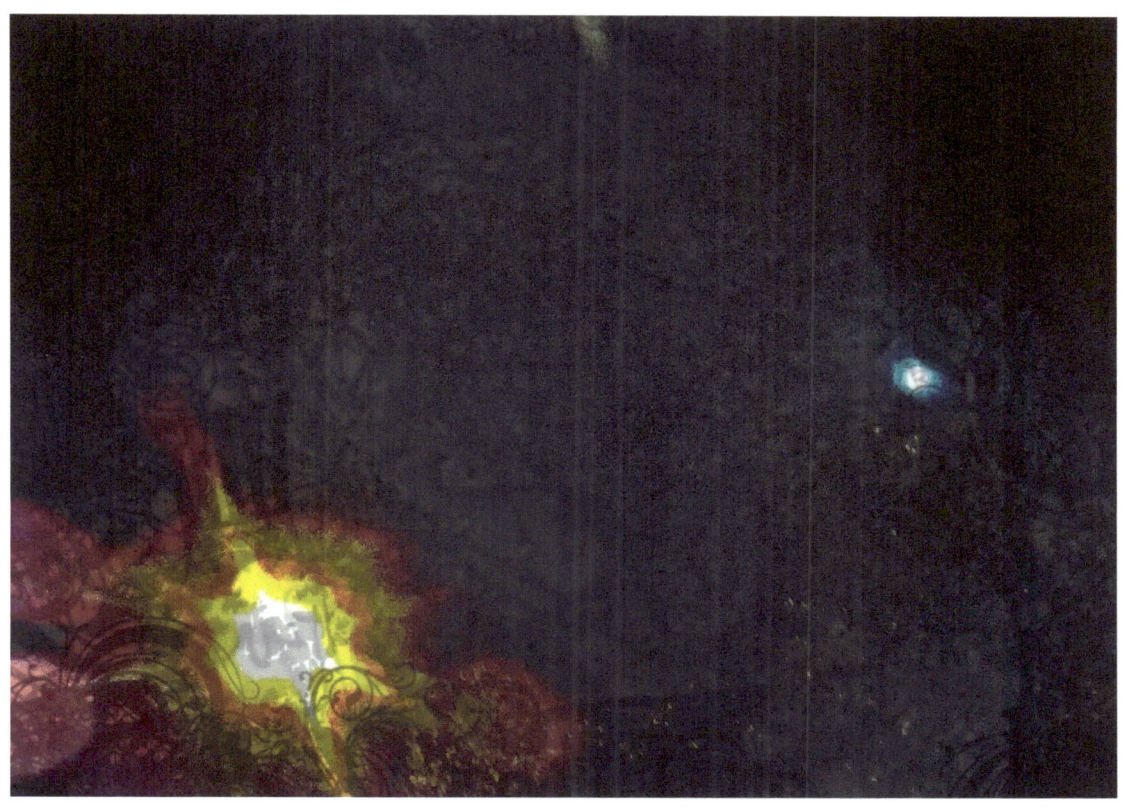

Flower moonlight

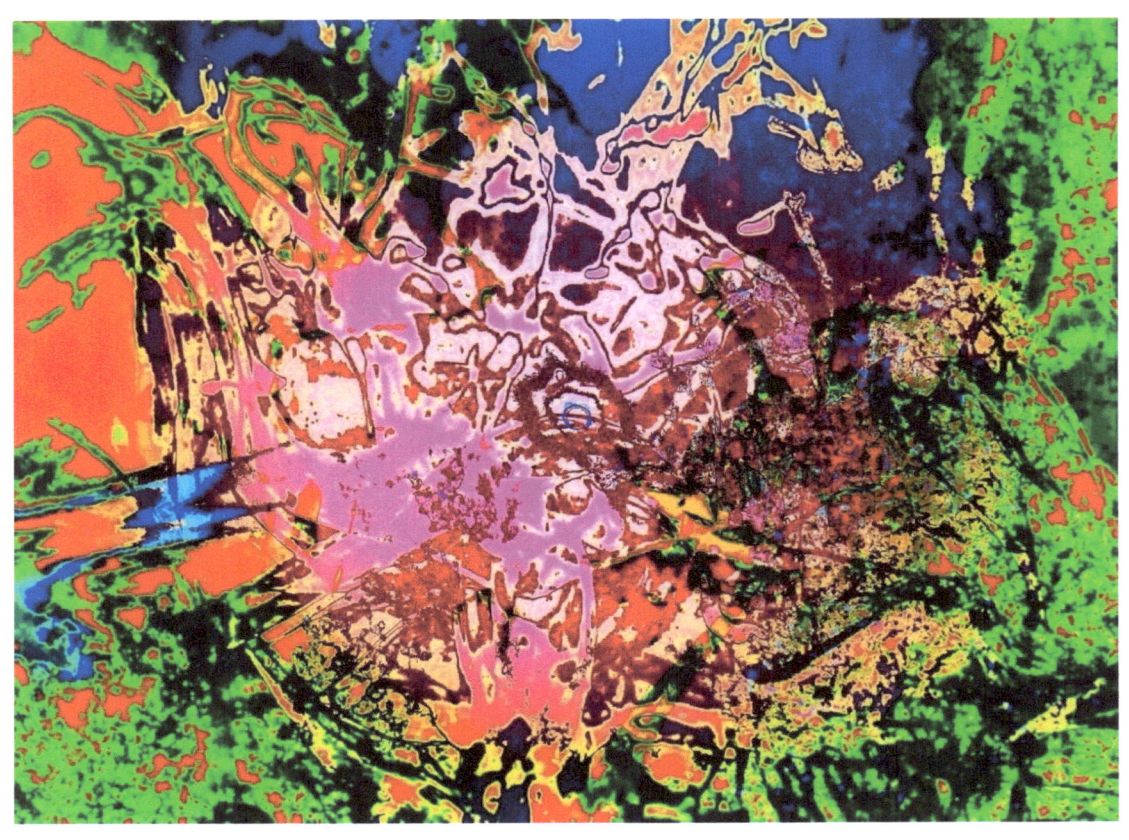

Fool moon' s happiness

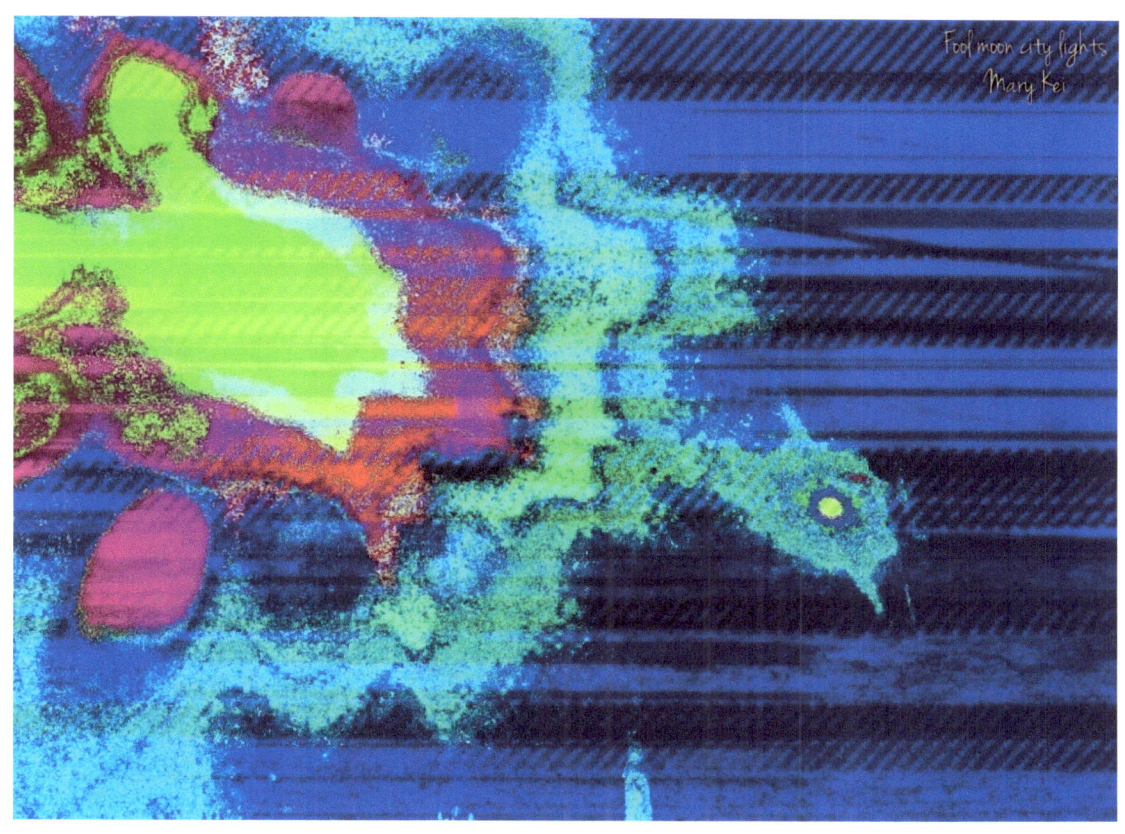

Fool moon city lights

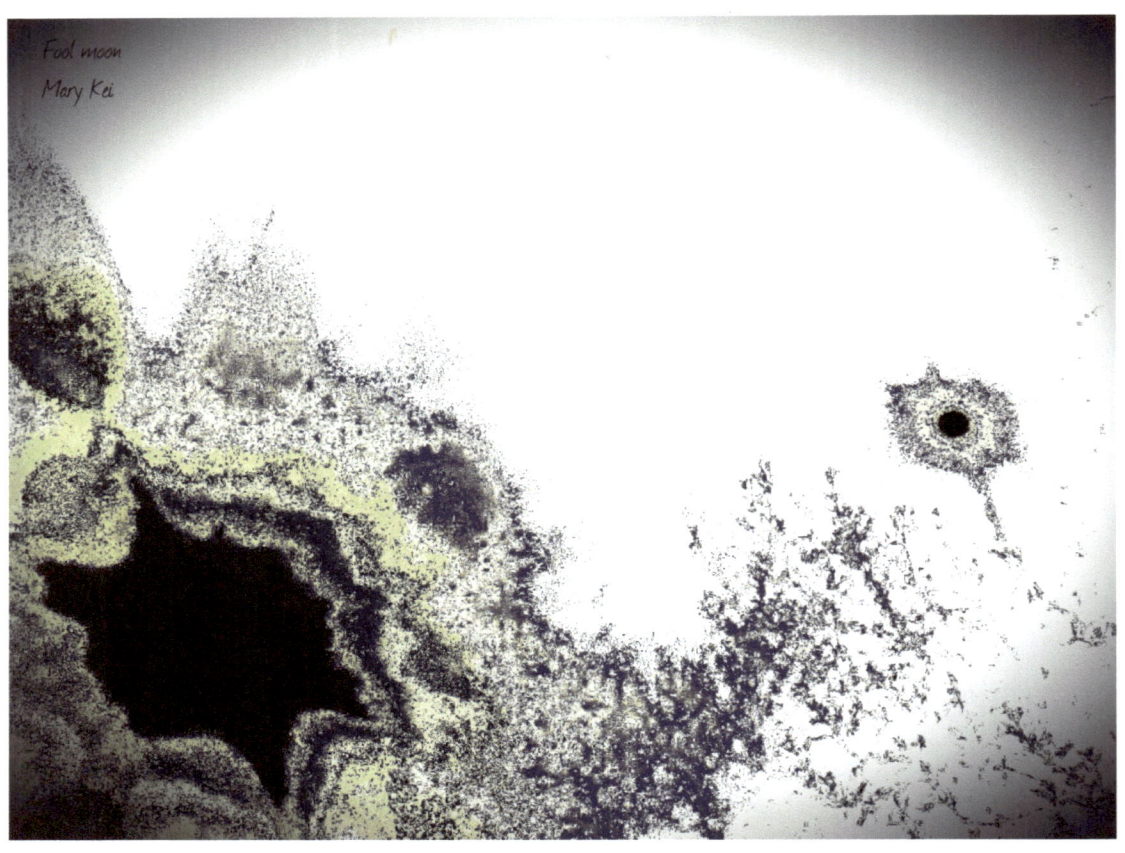

Flower moon

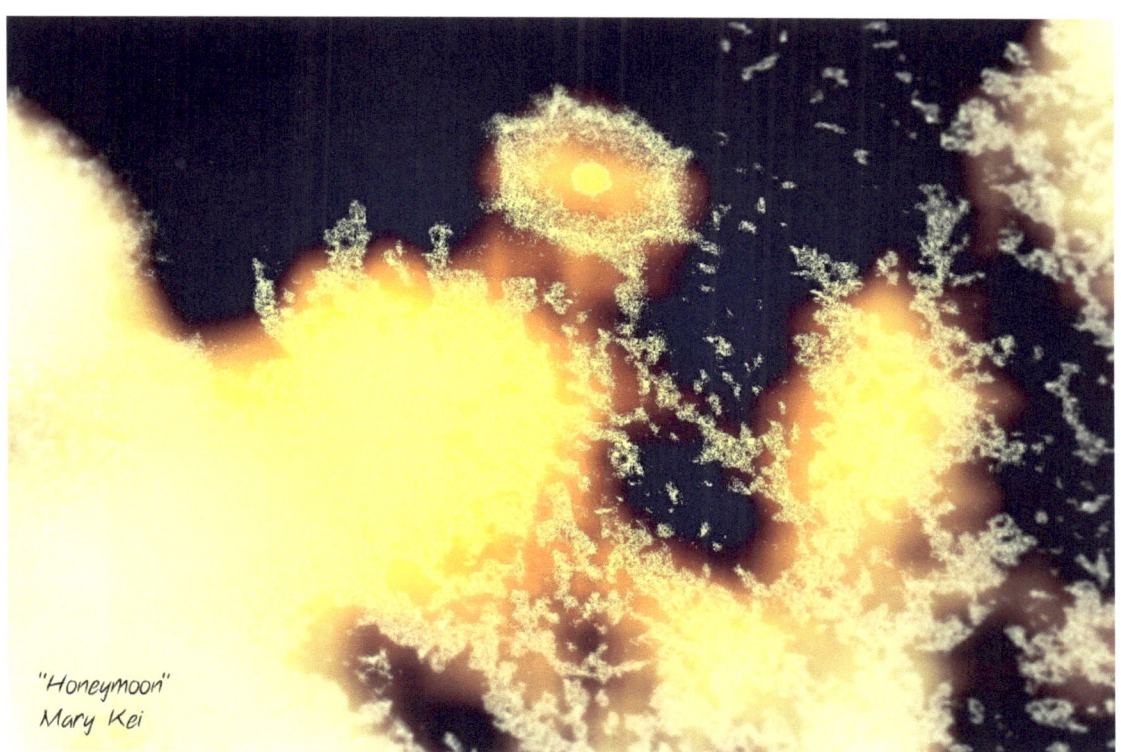

"Honeymoon"
Mary Kei

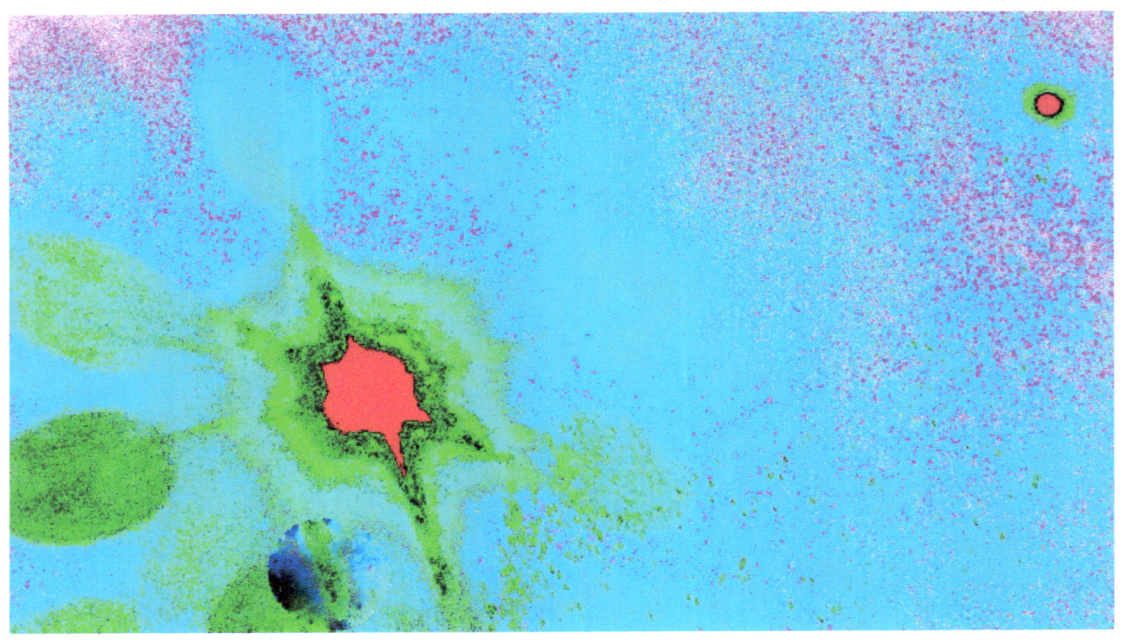

Flower moonlight

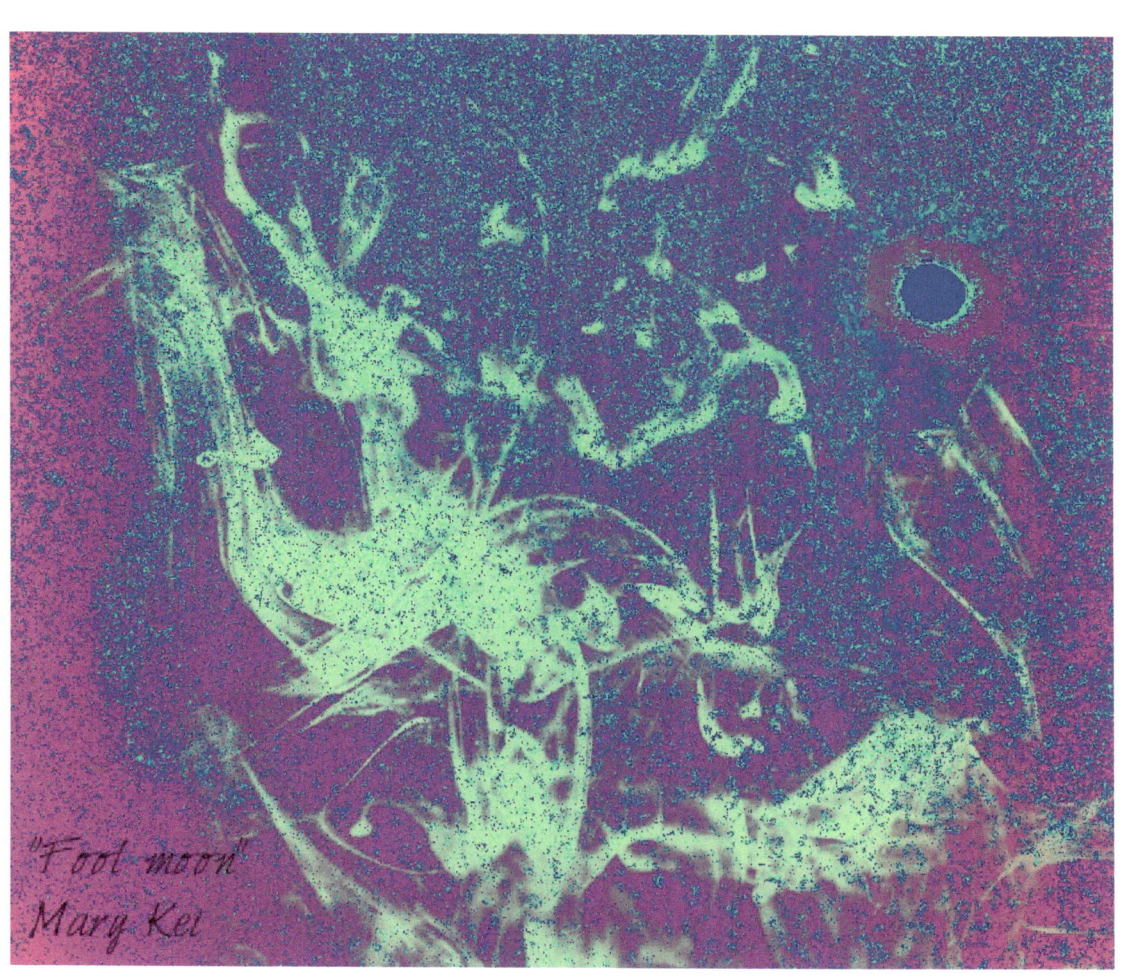

"Fool moon"
Mary Kei

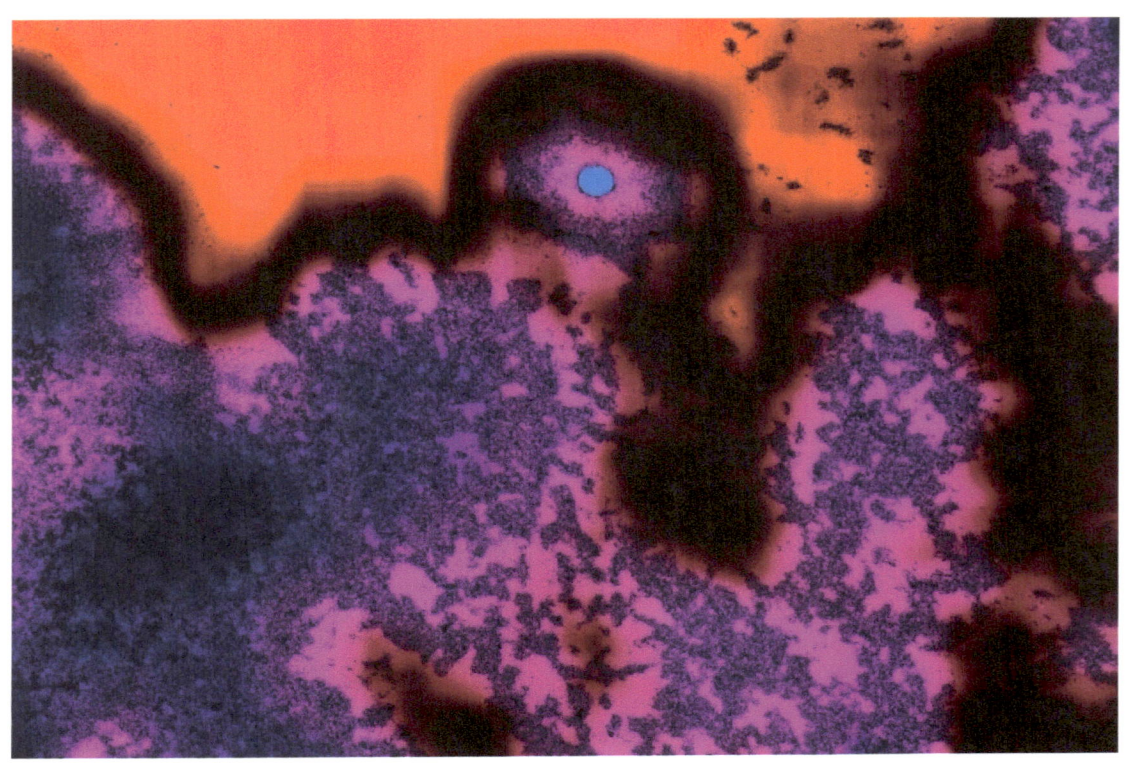

Moon shades

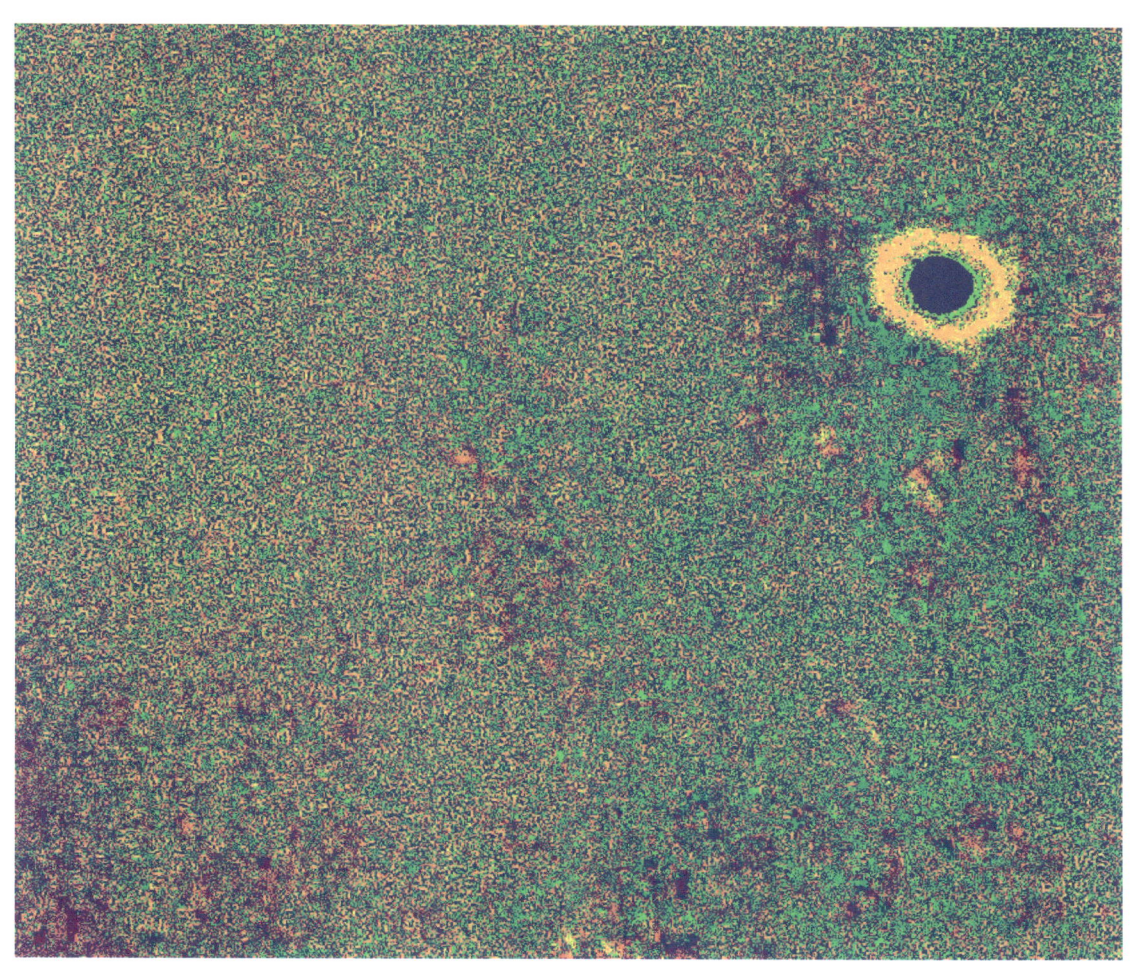

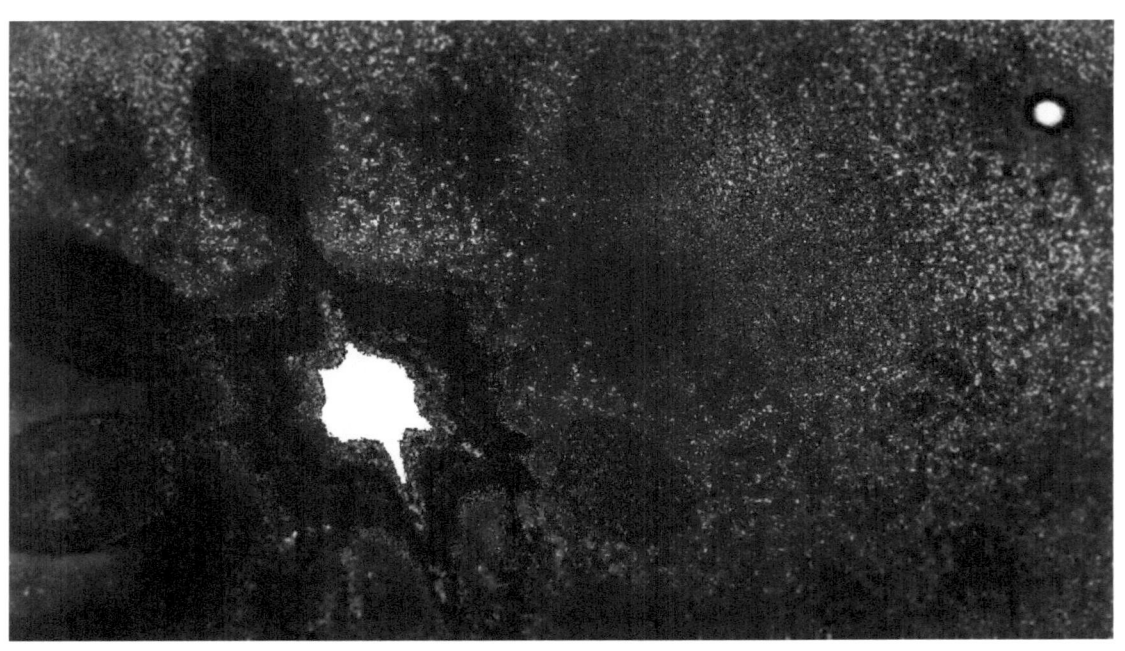

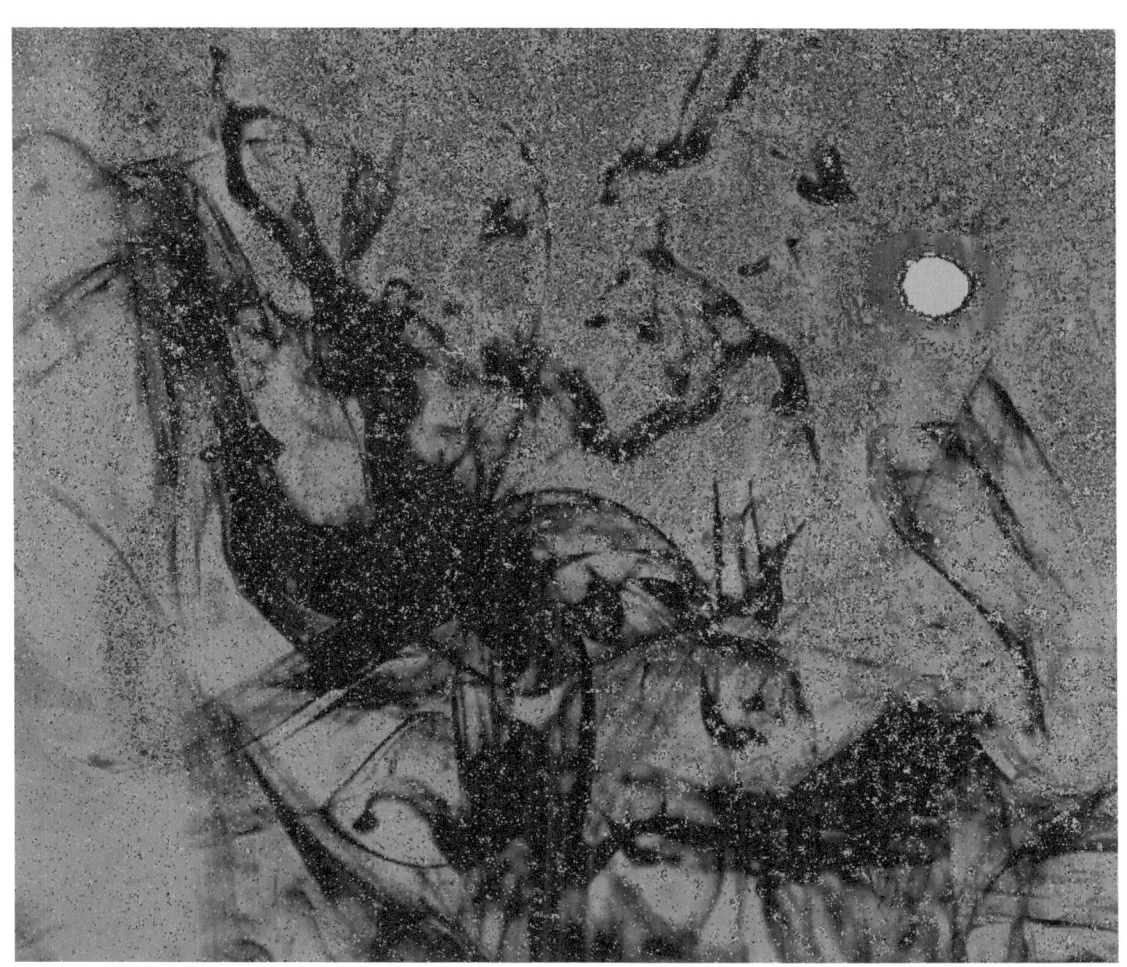

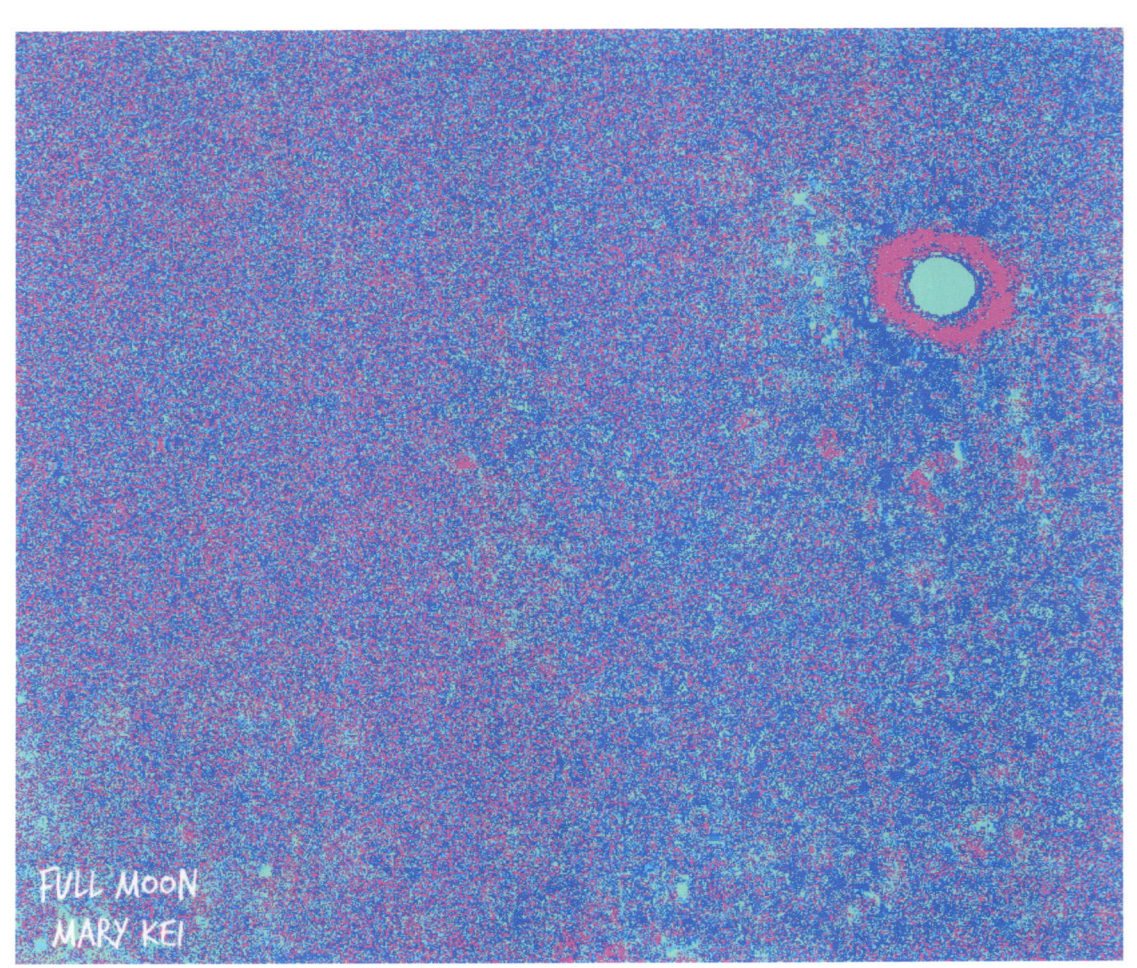

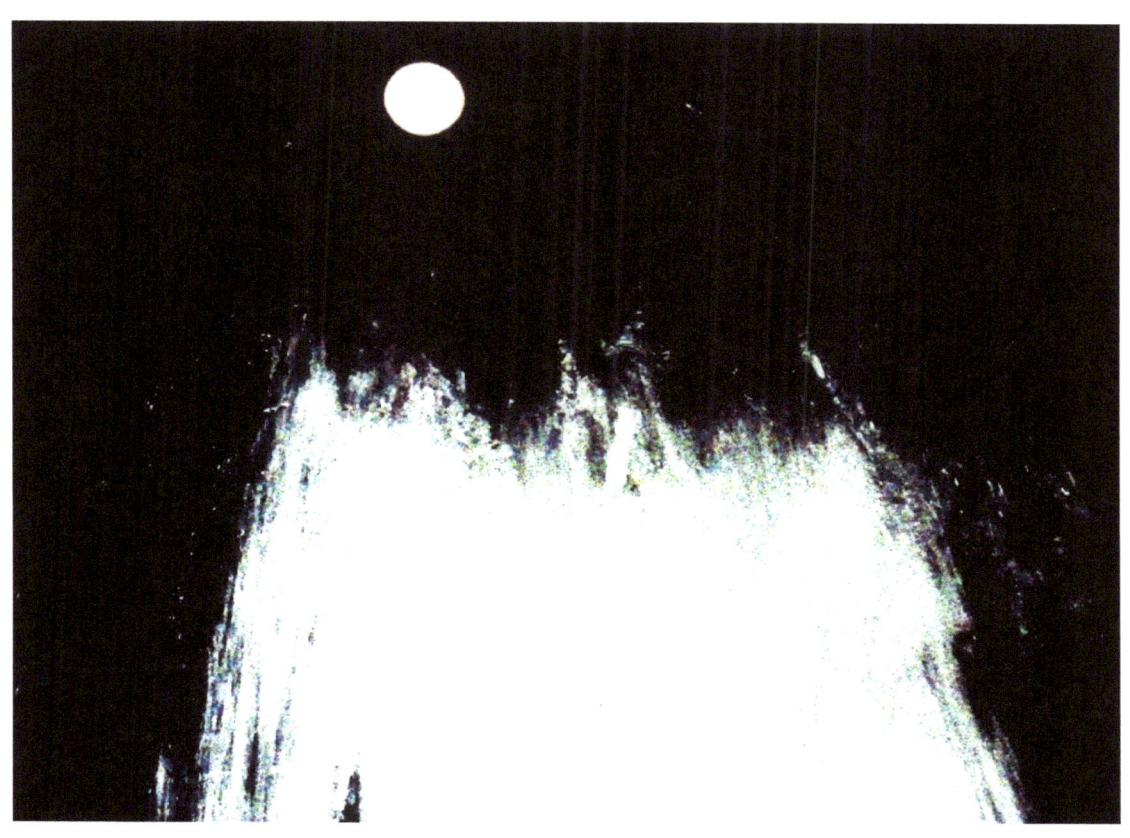

Fool moon

Syntagma Square
Athens

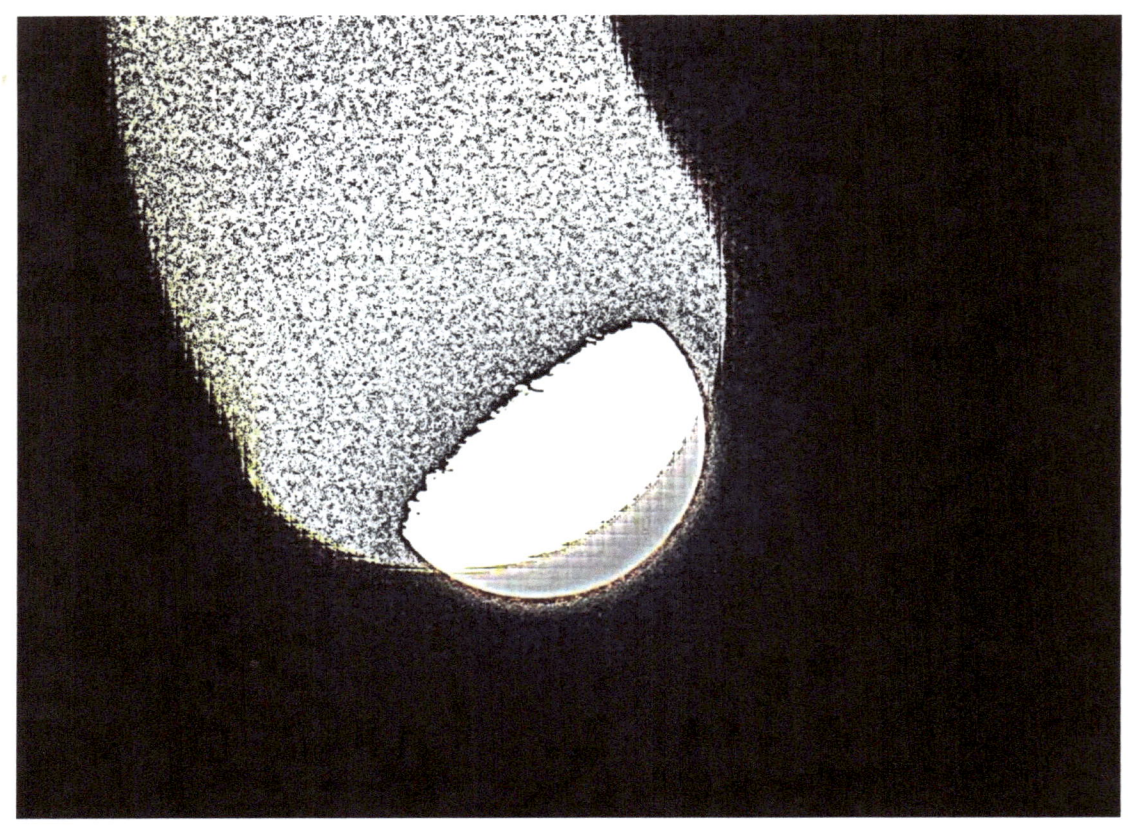

Falling moon

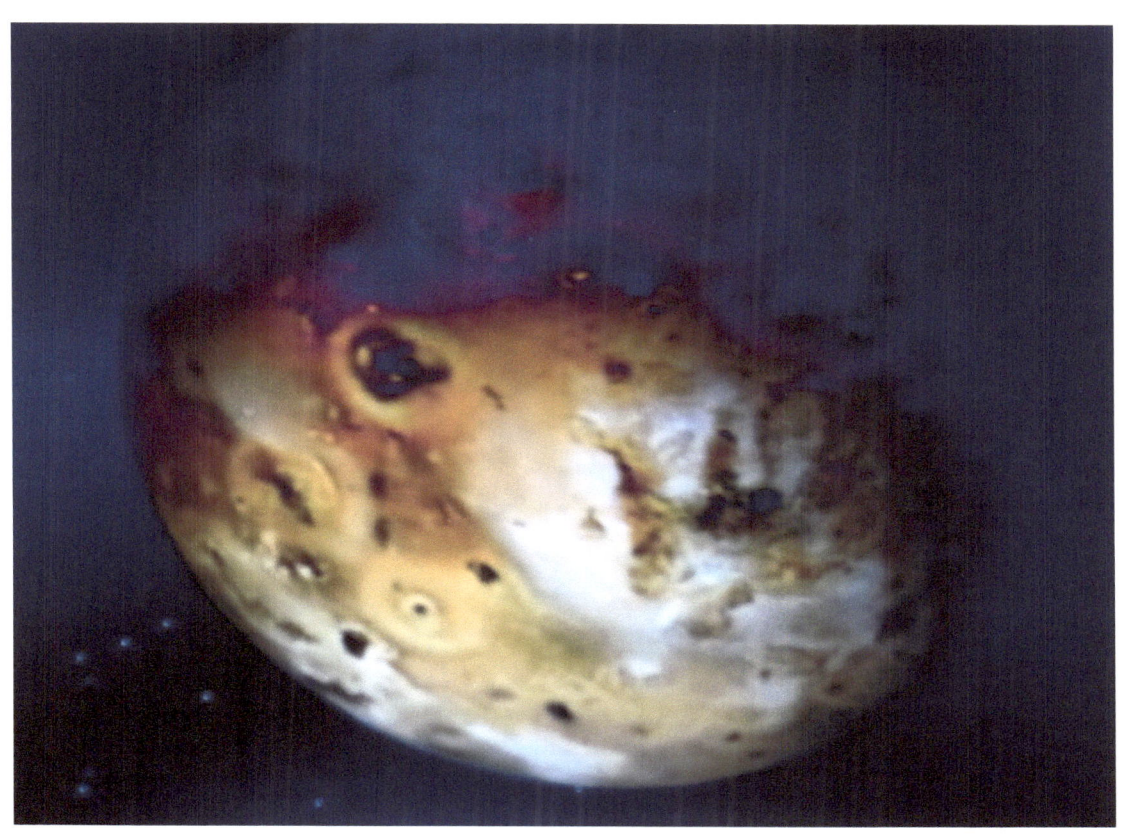

Io, Jupiter' s moon

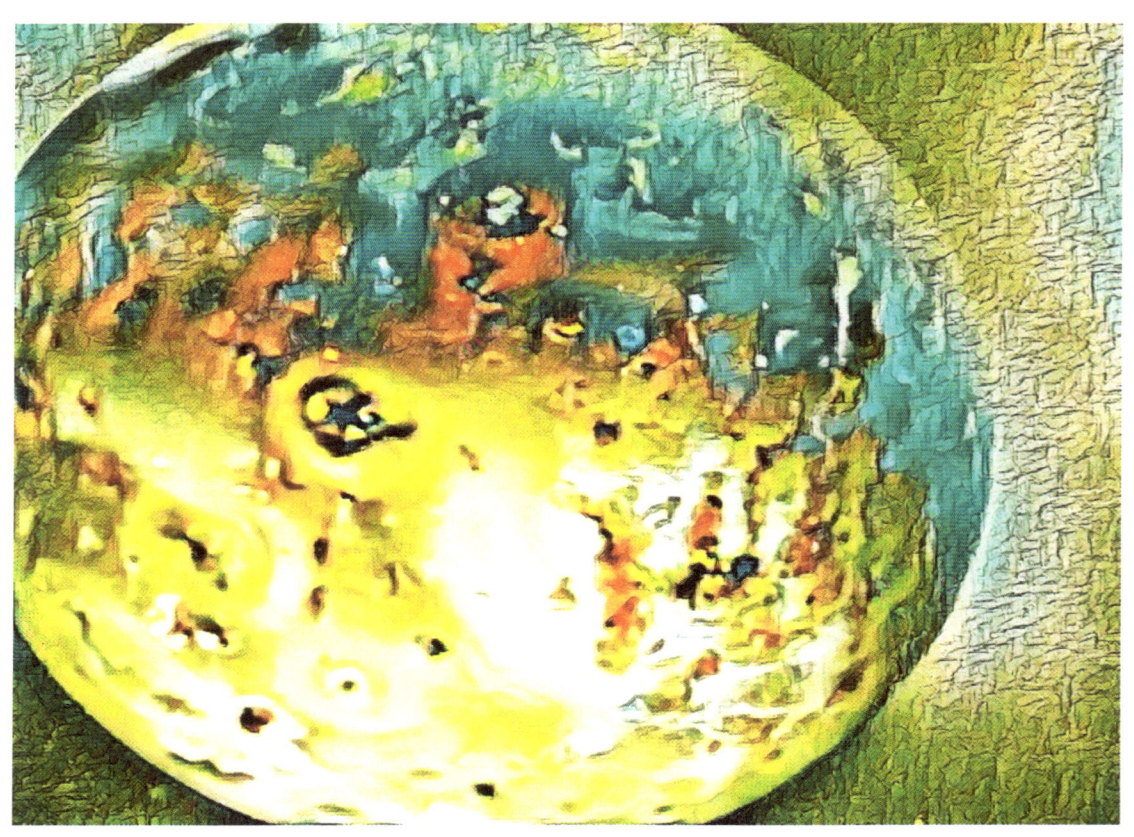

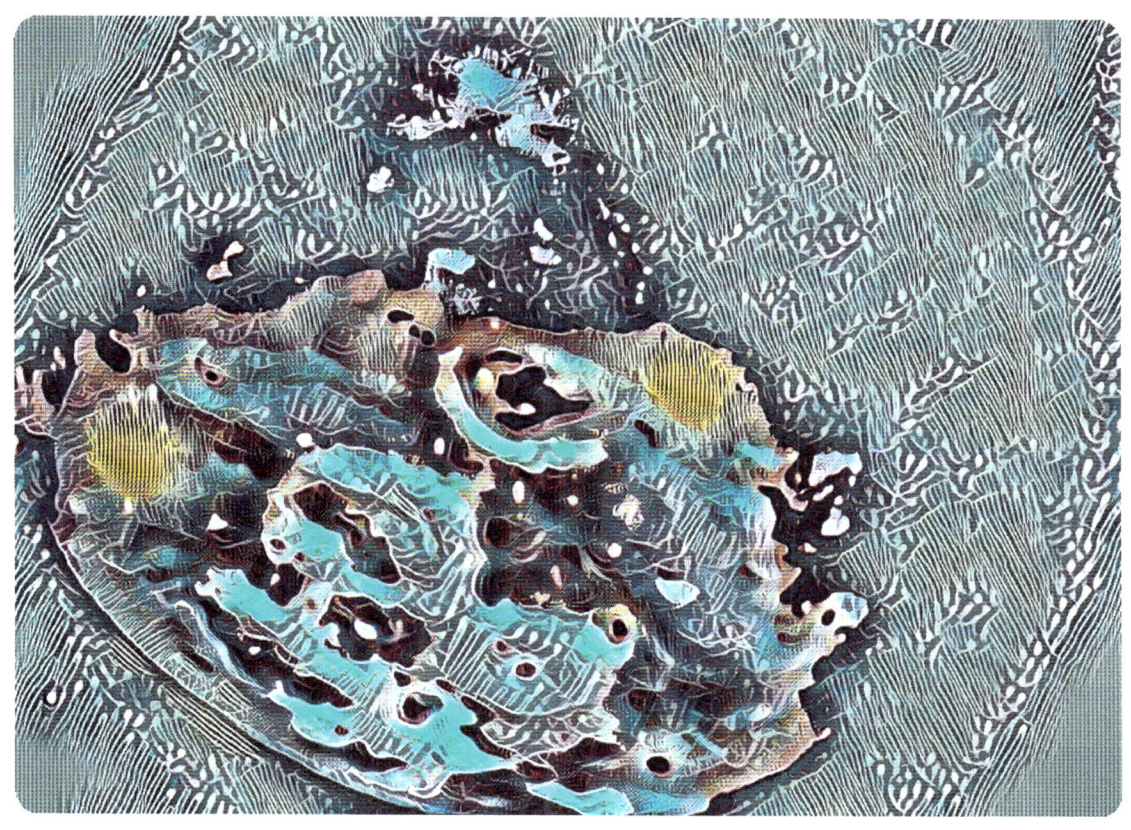

Io & Jupiter

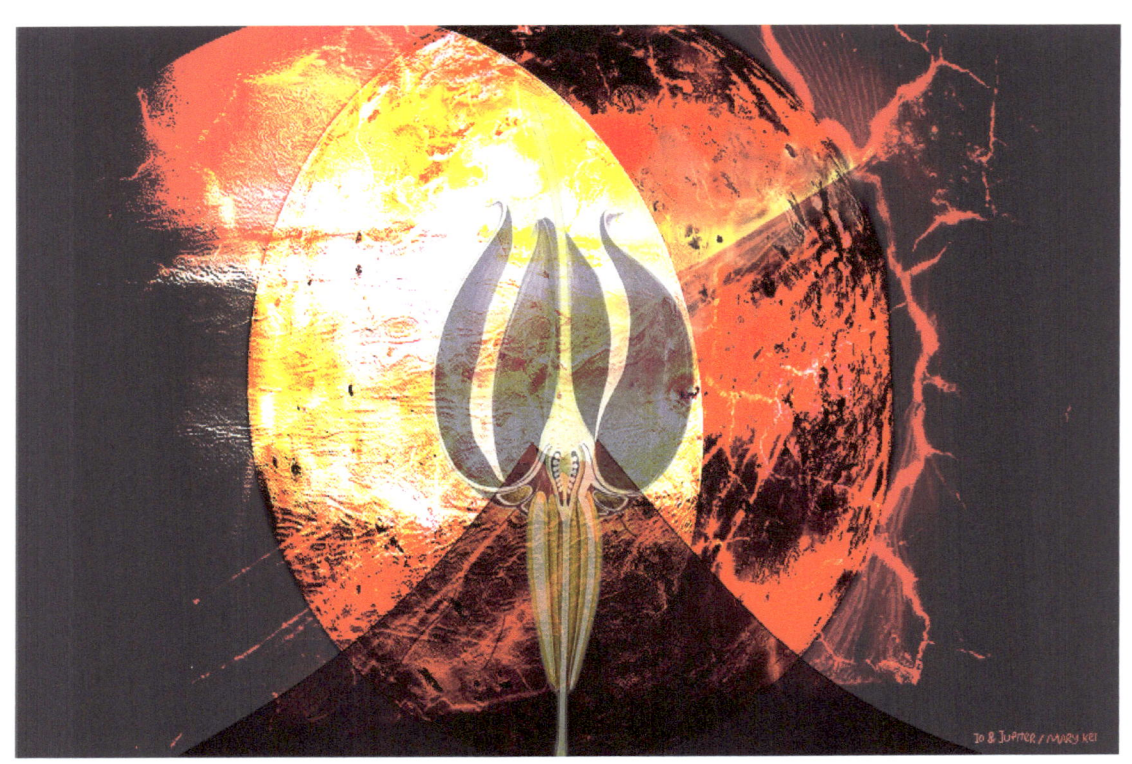

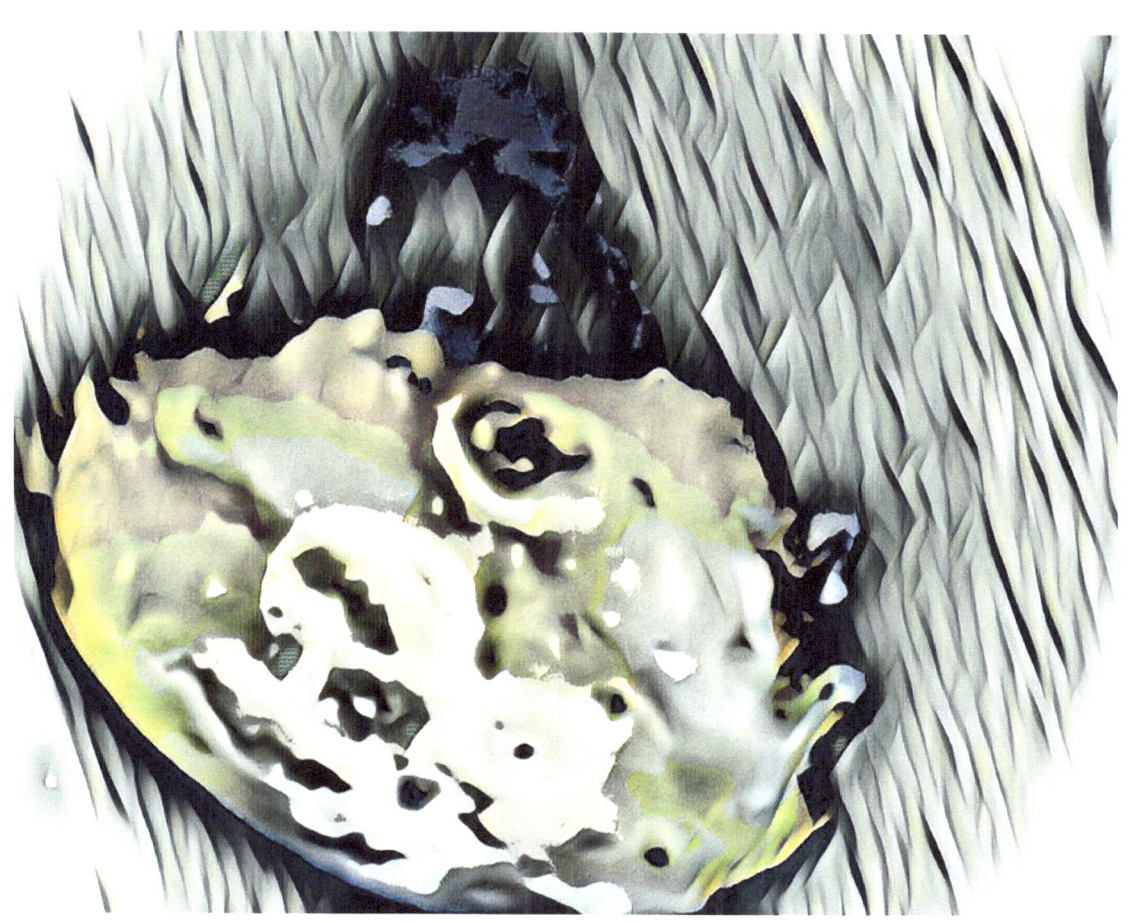

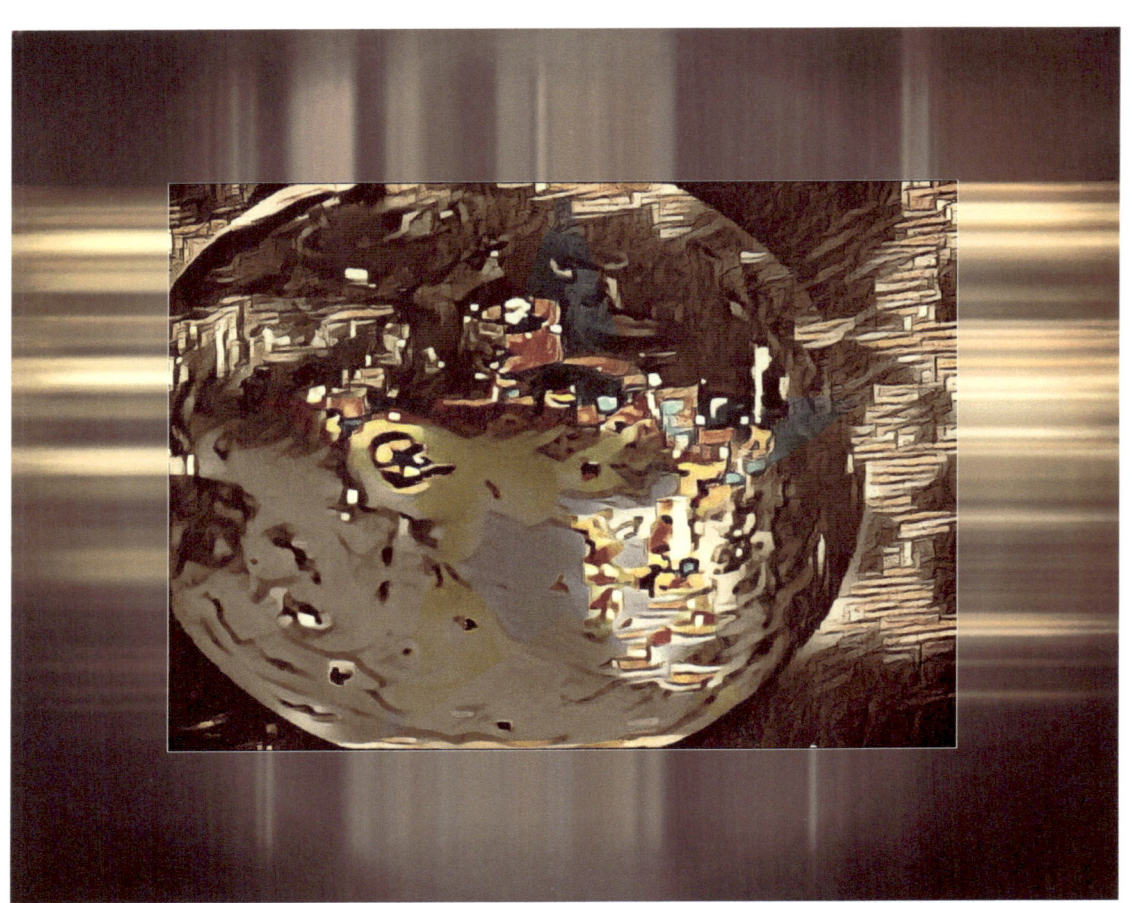

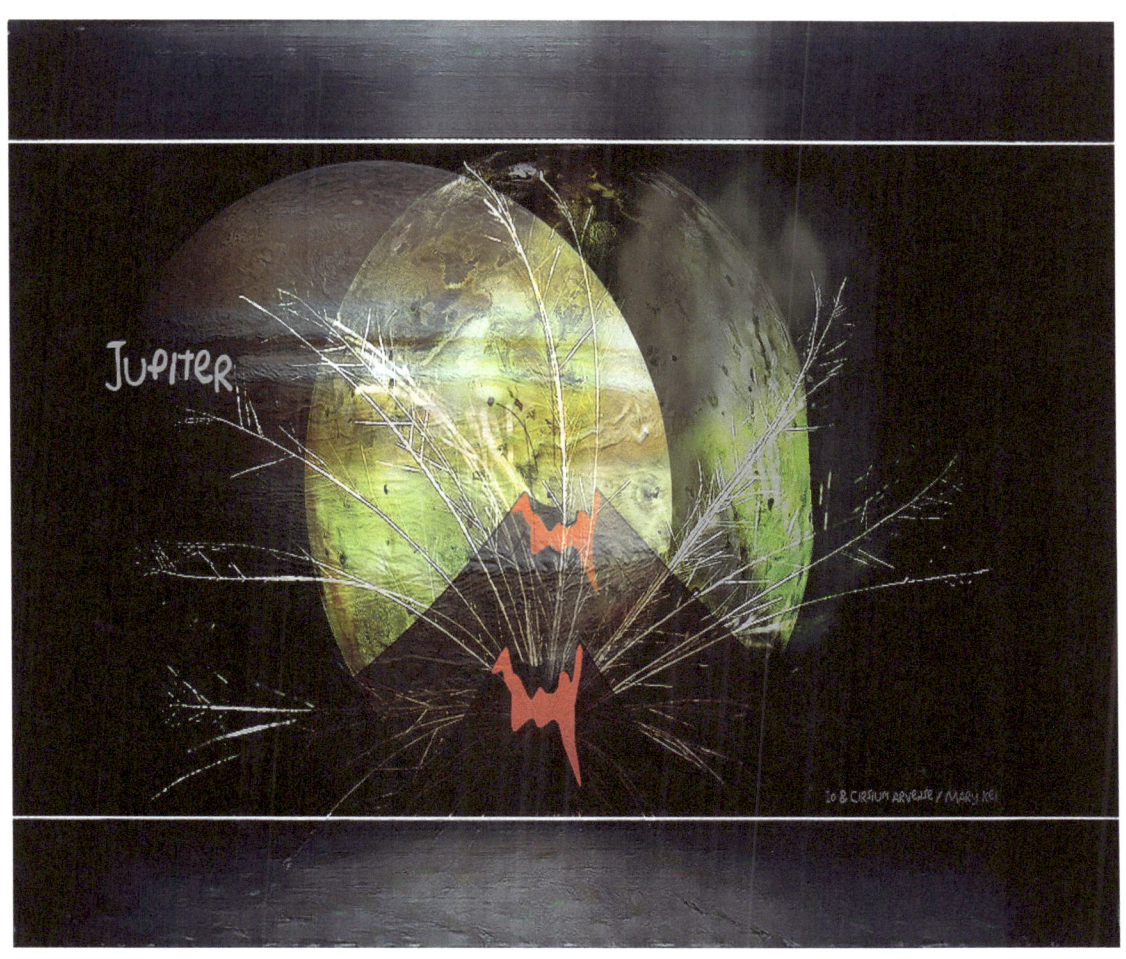

Io & Cirsium Arvense

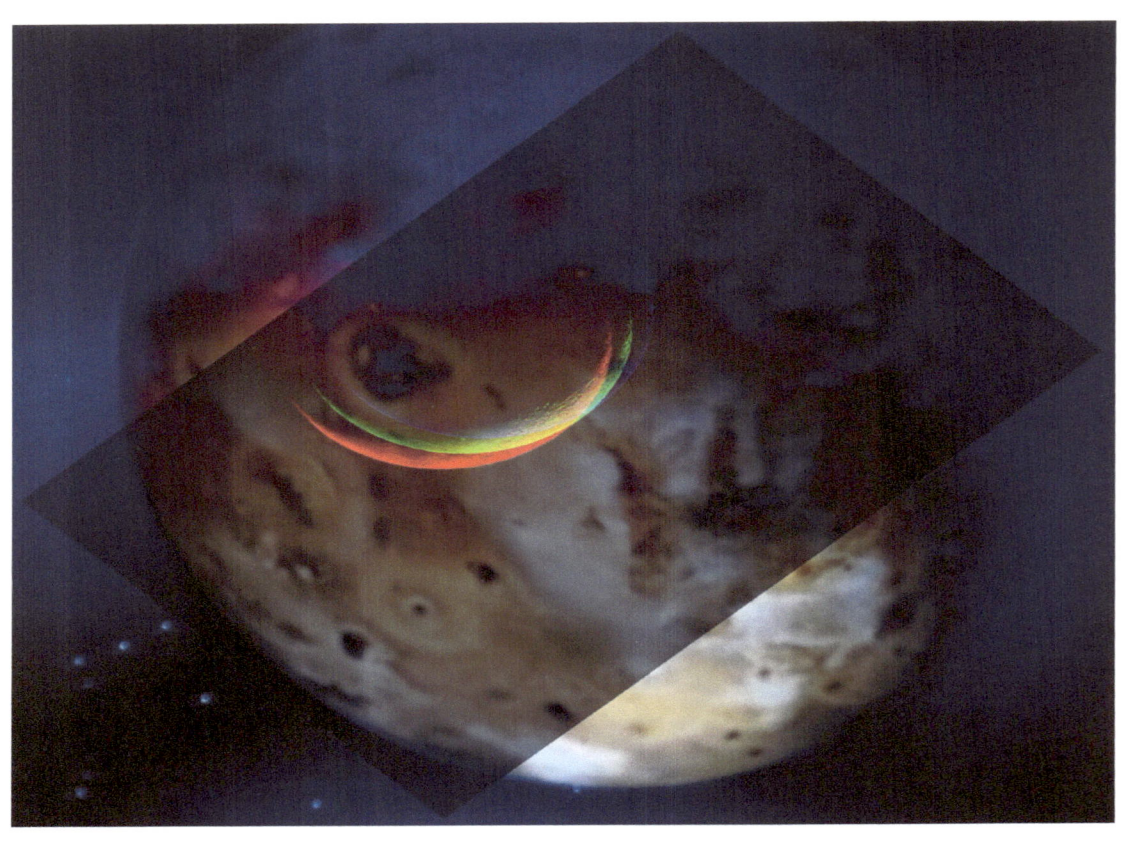

Io' s kaleidoscope

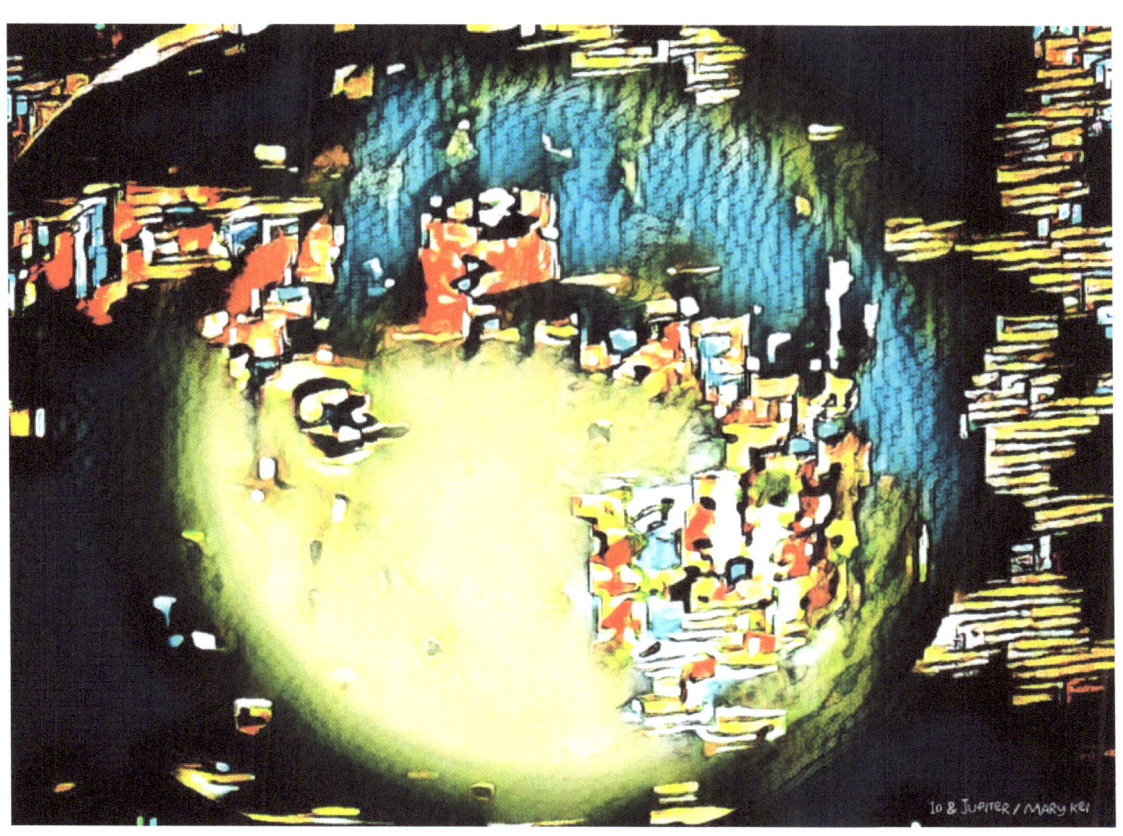

Io & Jupiter / MARY KEI

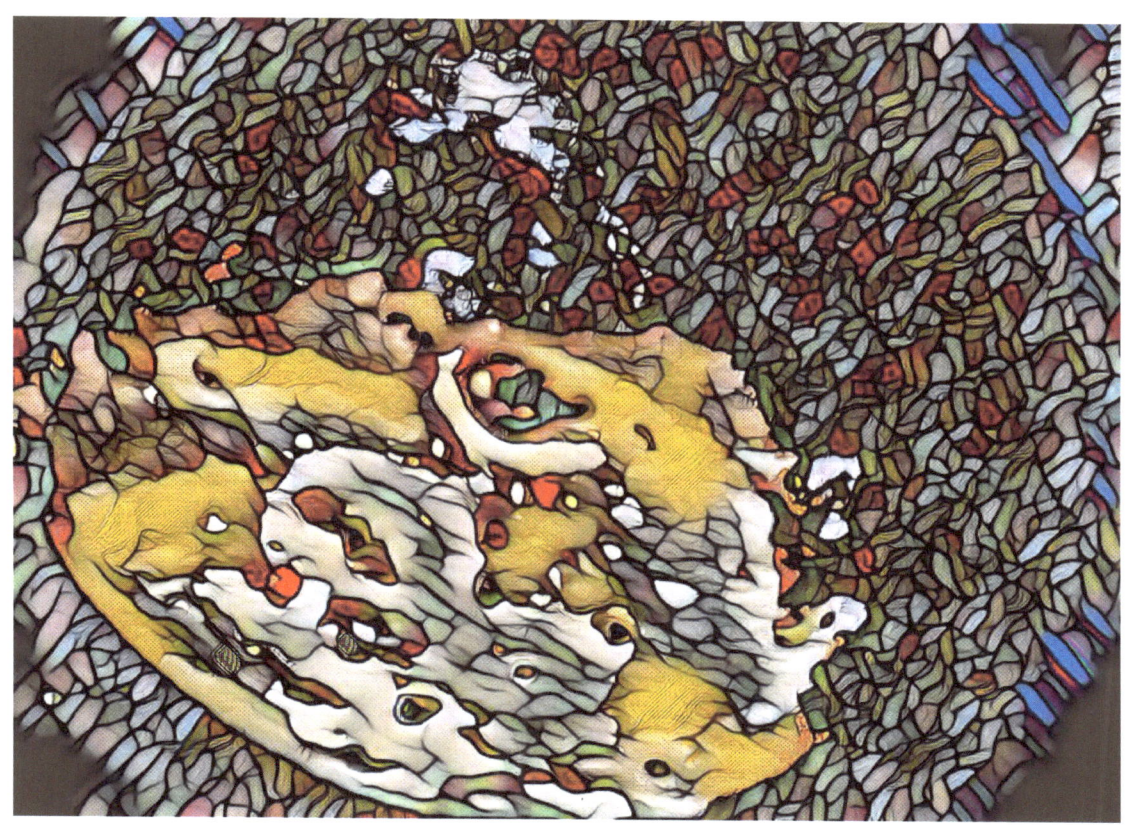

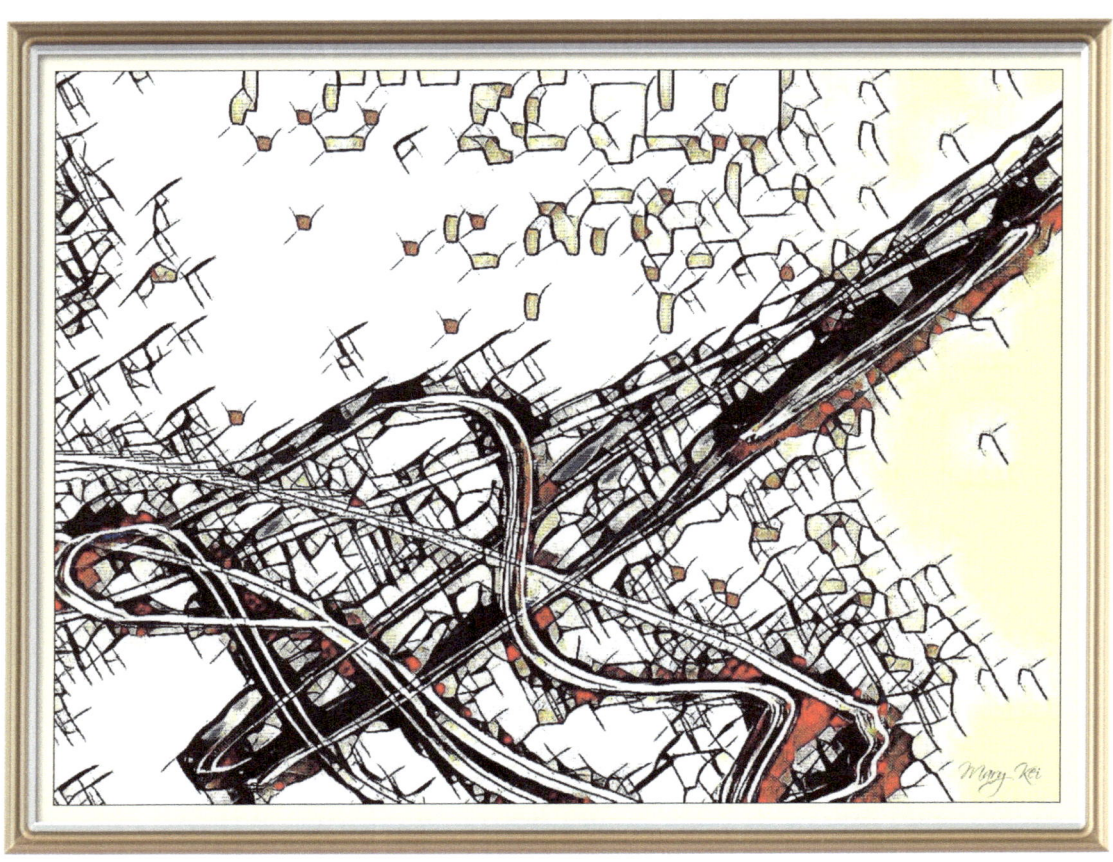

Aim for the moon

made by the moonlight

~~~

Fine Art Astrophotography

by

Maria Keisoglou
Nickname: Mary Kei